Annie Gray is a histori specialising in the history of food and dining in Britain from around 1600 to the present day. She is the author of *Victory in the Kitchen* and *The Greedy Queen*, among a number of other titles. An honorary research associate at the University of York and a Fellow of the Royal History Society, she has presented TV history documentaries including *Victorian Bakers* and *The Sweetmakers*, and is the resident food historian on BBC Radio 4's *The Kitchen Cabinet*. She lives in East Anglia.

AT

CHRISTMAS
WE FEAST

Festive Food Through the Ages

ANNIE GRAY

P

PROFILE BOOKS

This paperback edition first published in 2022

First published in Great Britain in 2021 by
PROFILE BOOKS LTD
29 Cloth Fair
London
ECIA 7JQ

www.profilebooks.com

10 9 8 7 6 5 4 3 2 1

Typeset in Fournier by MacGuru Ltd
Printed and bound in Great Britain by CPI Group (UK) Ltd, Croydon, CRO 4YY

The moral right of the author has been asserted.

A CIP catalogue record for this book is available from the British Library.

ISBN 978 1 78816 820 5
eISBN 978 1 78283 859 3

For KJ, Rich, Rebecca & M.
Because it really is all about the Georgian Christmas.

Contents

Recipe notes

All temperatures are given as conventional oven (top and bottom heat), as this is most useful for baking. For fan ovens, reduce the temperature by 20°C.

All eggs are UK medium, but large won't make a massive difference.

If possible, source high-welfare meat, preferably organic and (for beef) grass-fed. It's better for the environment and tends to taste better.

All ingredients are easily obtainable in the UK. Some may be more challenging elsewhere, but suet is available online or through a good butcher.

Suet is the hard fat around the kidneys of mammals – generally veal or beef suet was used in the past; modern suet is usually beef, but you can also get a vegetarian suet.

No, you can't replace the butter with margarine (except for the wartime cake).

I assume that if you have food intolerances or dietary preferences, you will have ample experience in adapting recipes for your own needs. I haven't tested any alternatives, though, so can't vouch for the tastiness of making vegan trifle from a recipe dependent on dairy. Sorry.

Many of the recipes are unashamedly full of sugar, fat and booze. It's Christmas. It only happens once a year (except if you are writing a book on it, in which case it's a good excuse to indulge in lovely things for a much longer time).

Before we start ...

'There is one day of the year where English cuisine unfurls all its banners and shows itself in its national colours. This day, waited for so impatiently by the biggest eaters as much as the small, is Christmas Day.'

In 1904 French chef Alfred Suzanne attempted to sum up the importance of Christmas in England to his fellow cooks. It was, he concluded, all about the food. There were 'hecatombes of turkey ... massacres of fat beef ... mountains of plum puddings and thickets of mince pies'. Whether you were destitute, poor, middle-class, or the richest lord in the land, you aimed to feast, to have a meal beyond the ordinary, made up, on this one day, of a list of foods so specific to the English Christmas that they were scarcely seen at any other time of the year.[1]

Suzanne was writing at the end of the Victorian era, which we see now as one of the defining periods of the British Christmas. But the Victorians saw the late Tudors as having defined Christmas, with their own modifications merely returning it to where it belonged.

No one era invented Christmas. No one person changed the way it was celebrated. How it is seen, and the rituals which surround it, have evolved, and, while it's true that much of the surface paraphernalia of the modern Christmas can be ascribed to one or two decades (mainly the 1840s), there are deeper themes which cross the centuries.

Feasting is one of them. We rarely feast now in the old sense, with connotations of hospitality and invited guests eating lavishly at our expense, opting for a more practical modern version, pared back to a few lucky diners, eating lots of food beyond the ordinary. We have eaten and drunk to excess in the middle of winter since before Christmas was a word, and it seems entirely probable that we will continue to do so for as long as we can. But although it can seem otherwise, the things we consume are not set in stone. Our dinners have evolved as much as the context in which we eat them.

Nostalgia, tradition and a sense of time-honoured ritual surround Christmas dinner. We only eat it once a year, so it is unsurprising that its evolution is slow. It plays a marked role in the way in which we build and maintain our relationships, so it is equally unsurprising that we might not want to change it. But for something so many people love, and look forward to, it can be a gargantuan amount of work, out of all proportion to the normal rhythm of cooking and eating. It is also lopsided in terms of workload – women do most of the cooking – and often fraught with tension as families come together at a time of enormous social pressure compounded by immediate, dinner-related, stress. And yet the love we feel is genuine, the warm and fuzzy feelings real, and the work and indigestion – usually – worth it.

Every family has its own culinary Christmas customs, joined haphazardly to wider cultural norms. But while we might think we know the origins of what we eat, the stories around Christmas food are confused and murky. Myths cluster thickly around Christmas in general, and there are many attached to its foods. But whether it's the number of ingredients in a Christmas pudding, the shape of a mince pie, or the exact date a pair of breeding turkeys first set foot on British shores, all crumble in the face of logic.

This book is an exploration of the history of the dishes and ingredients that we associate with Christmas: where they came from, how we've prepared them, and how they've come to be part of so many people's Christmases. I've drawn on recipe books, menus, fiction, diaries, newspapers and visual depictions of food and feasting at Christmas. Writing down a recipe doesn't mean it was ever cooked, of course, just as descriptions of meals aren't necessarily accurate. We all edit our own stories, as well as those of others, and recipe writing is as much a form of storytelling as anything else. But when recipes are repeated, in book after book (sometimes verbatim), and tales are told that tally closely with each other, it does add up to a rich and fascinating history.

This is the story of the British Christmas, which, in practice, means the English Christmas. By the late eighteenth century, it was recognised by both the English and those abroad as distinct from that of any other country. Both in a general sense and a culinary one, it was explicitly tied to notions of Englishness, and proudly promoted as something unique. When the English colonised other countries, they took their Christmas with them, spreading it across the globe in determined ignorance of any local customs or other sensitivities. By the twentieth century its foods were largely regarded as English oddities, embraced as such by those who were aware that this was true, but more often seen as simply normal and universal by those who ate them. Surely everyone, everywhere, spent December in anticipation of their annual plum pudding?

Christmas feasting was, from the outside, remarkably uniform, but viewed from within it has never really been so. Class and wealth have always played a huge role in defining what is eaten for dinner. Regionality once played a role, too.

The foods you'll find here are those which repeated polls suggest are our festive favourites. Sadly, you won't necessarily find everything you most crave at Christmas, or the things your family can't do without. You won't find sections on nuts, or oranges, or sugar mice, for although all of these are part of many Christmases, they are not unique to the season, and don't feature anywhere near the top of lists of Christmas food. I've also resisted the lure of some of the modern abominations, including Brussels sprout vodka, mince-pie flavour pork sausages and mint choc chip pringles (really, don't). But you will find contextualising sections showing how

Christmas dinners have changed, as well as recipes drawn from the past which deserve to be more widely known.

The story of Christmas foods is both global and local, riven by class differences even while appearing to be a cross-cultural norm. And it continues to evolve. We cling to Christmas dinner as a point of stability even as our culinary tastes expand, but it's built on shifting sands. So, let's look again at the foods we think of as festive, let's consider why we love them, and maybe add a touch of the past to Christmases yet to come.

The Twelve Days: merriment, mischief and mirth

Everything has to start somewhere. In the case of Christmas, it was in the fourth century, when the early Christian Church adopted the period around late December and early January as the time for celebrating the birth of Christ. In doing so it harnessed a broad-ranging set of existing traditions, most of which focused on lighting fires, feasting and drinking. It was the quietest time of the year for farming, thus lending itself to time off. The word Christmas was first recorded much later, in the eleventh century. Two centuries after that, there were already complaints that it was a season of gluttony, groping and having far too much to drink.

Throughout its history the celebratory side of the season has always triumphed over the religious side.[2] That's not to say the religious observance didn't matter, but the Christian Church (or most of its denominations) pragmatically took the view that wild partying and gustatory enjoyment was all part of the festival. It meant that Christmas was highly successful and widely observed. As a universal festival, it also meant that it quickly became seen as highly traditional, with certain themes – notably hospitality, goodwill and making merry – embedded within it from very early on.

The medieval Christmas contained many elements we'd recognise today, including carols, plays and time off work. It was built around the Twelve Days, which in Britain ran from December 25th through to the Feast of the Epiphany on the 5th of January (it's a grey area; sometimes they go from December 26th to January 6th). Each of the days had a particular importance, from St Stephen's Day on the 26th, to the Feast of the Holy Innocents on the 28th and the Feast of St Thomas Becket on the 29th. The 1st of January was both the pre-Christian New Year's Day and the Feast of the Circumcision. Some days were fixed across the Catholic Church, others were more local and obscure. In theory, no work was done, and those who could afford it threw open their doors and feasted all and sundry.

The feast element was particularly welcome, coming as it did at the end of a long and dreary period of fast. Advent then was one of the two big fast periods, when no animal-derived products could be consumed. It was twenty-four days of fish, vegetables and almond milk (the latter proving there is little truly new in food, handy tetrapack cartons aside). As ever, the rich transformed their (fresh) produce with spices, imported fruit and nuts and clever cooking, while the less wealthy subsisted on preserved produce, including stockfish, which needed soaking and hammering over several days to tenderise it and make it edible. For the poor, fasting probably made little difference, since the staple diet contained very little meat anyway, revolving instead around bread, pulses and vegetables – but they would have missed vital protein from milk, cheese and eggs. The rich, meanwhile, put on lavish fish feasts. One fifteenth-century menu included porpoise and peas, baked lamprey, turbot, cream of almond pottage and a satisfyingly large range of fruits in syrup, wafers and almond milk jellies.[3]

Fasting was a huge part of the pre-Reformation Catholic calendar, and over half of the days of the year were nominated as fast days – Wednesdays, Fridays and Saturdays, plus Lent, as well as Advent – and various other days as well. You could get around the restrictions if you were ill or very young or old, while others paid fines and ate meat anyway. For the Church this could be a valuable source of revenue – Rouen Cathedral's butter tower was paid for with money from otherwise illicit butter-eating in Lent.[4] The royal court led by example by being decidedly lax about the whole thing, especially on Wednesdays. There were also oddities which counted as fish, such as barnacle geese (they hang out on water), beavers' tails (scaly), puffins (dive) and seals (not sure but look fishy), which were deemed to be seafood. However, for most people meat was off the menu. As habitual as it might have been, it was still a hardship, at least for the poor:

We ate no puddings nor no sauce,
But stinking fish not worth a louse …
There was no fresh fish far not near,
Salt fish and salmon was too dear …
Our bread was brown, our ale was thin,
Our bread was musty in the bin.[5]

Add to that the general hideousness of the English winter, and it was little wonder that when the 25th finally arrived, people went a little crazy.

For the rich, the Twelve Days really were time off, as well as time to show off. Lords of Misrule were appointed to mastermind upper-class festivities, which often centred on turning society a little topsy-turvy – appointing boy-bishops to read sermons, for example – but there was plenty of more plebeian misrule as well. Troops of mummers performed plays, generally noisy and happily bawdy, and costumes were very much the order of the day. Then there was the eating. There are records of some gargantuan feasts. In 1213 the court of King John took delivery of 24 hogsheads of wine, 200 heads of pork, 50lb of pepper, 2lb of saffron and 15,000 herrings, among a vast array of other things. No foods were exclusive to Christmas, although by the sixteenth century some were certainly associated with it. They were almost all expensive – thus good for showing largesse and status – or seasonal. Most were both.

At the upper end of society meals were served as two main courses. Each consisted of a large number of dishes, the contents of which were restricted by sumptuary law. These laws, which were largely abolished in England in the seventeenth century, aimed to regulate spending on luxuries, encourage key industries, and enforce rank, by dictating what any given person could wear and eat according to their status. They were widely flouted and, as with fast days for the Church, became a source of tax for the government, as people paid fines to get around them. But they are very useful in showing what was deemed a luxury for rich Tudors, apparently all desperate to show off by the size of their ruff.

Meals might well be broken up with a bit of performance art. In Stirling in 1594, guests at the Christening Feast of Prince Henry were treated between courses to a 24ft-long model ship surrounded by women dressed as sirens and staffed with burly silk-clad sailors. The ship's cargo was spectacular sugarcraft – sugar oysters, limpets, whitings, herrings, all 'most lively represented in their own shape'.[6] At the end of dinner, selected dignitaries were treated to more sugar in a final course, known in the medieval era as the 'void', but by the sixteenth century usually called the banqueting course.

The banqueting course was often held in a separate room, or banqueting house. It was all about the sugar: sugar sculptures, moulded sugar, plus a selection of sweet, expensive titbits eaten as a palate cleanser. These included gingerbread, candied fruit, fruit in syrup, marmalades, biscuits, wafers and comfits. All were ostensibly digestives, but all were increasingly eaten mainly for pleasure, and gained a reputation for hedonism and sexual licentiousness – inevitable with all those sticky fingers and delicate little treats flavoured with hot spices (although in reality the banqueting course was the only situation where forks were used before they spread to the main part of dinner in the mid-seventeenth century).

The remains of meals were reused or distributed to members of the household or the poor. Feeding the poor was a significant part of the duties of a large house more generally, not just at Christmas, but the season did carry with it an extra expectation of generosity. The hospitable ideal was of an open house, and some establishments did practise this right up to the eve of the Civil War. In 1624 the Archbishop of York held six huge Christmas feasts, feeding hundreds of his parishioners, and there are many examples of landowners holding smaller feasts for their tenants and dependants in the area. But such events were not open to all, rather to those with a relationship to the feast-giver, and the arrangements were often reciprocal. Christmas was well established as a time for gift-giving, and edible gifts were expected from tenant to landlord. Meanwhile, extra beer, beef and fuel went the other way, part of the highly intertwined nature of relations in a pre-industrial society.

Even after the Reformation in the 1540s, the English Christmas remained essentially that of the medieval era. Henry VIII made few changes, apart from banning the Feast of Thomas Becket on December 29th (celebrating a man who stood against royal authority was intolerable). Edward VI, meanwhile, changed misrule and mummers to more organised masques, the start of a steady process of taming the season, which, outside all the eating, was also an excuse for social upheaval, riotous partying and football (some things don't change). But by the end of the century Christmas had changed, both in broad terms and in culinary ones.

By the beginning of the seventeenth century there were clearly identifiable Christmas foods. Boar's head was one, brawn was another. It was joined by Christmas pies, which were sometimes mince pies, sometimes enormous game pies, but quickly the former gained their own, definite identity. Ben Jonson, in a Christmas masque of 1616, included characters called Minced Pie, Wassail and Baby Cake. The latter was another name for Twelfth Cake, while wassail was a drink whose ingredients varied wildly, but was invariably alcoholic.

Plum pottage, too, made an appearance by name, predated by similar variously named dishes which shared with it rich, spicy flavours and a mixture of meat and dried fruit. Farmed fowl was present in many lists of Christmas fare, and included turkey, goose, capon (castrated chicken) and swan. Turkey, swan and peacock were all true feast birds – big, hard to obtain and with impressive plumage. They could be roasted, head and legs on, but were more impressive as a pie, with the body made from pastry and the fully-feathered head, wings and tail gently baked on skewers to be stuck in the pie. Meat was prestigious and unobtainable for much of the populace, so it was unsurprising that it was in demand. One writer ruefully commented that 'Capons and hennes, besides turkies, geese and duckes, besides beefe and mutton, all die for the great feast, for in twelve days a multitude of people will not bee fed with a little.'[7]

As the Tudor dynasty gave way to the Stuarts, and James I of England and VI of Scotland brought these two nations together under his reign, Christmas was thriving. But there were mutterings that it thrived a bit too much. While the vast majority of people looked forward to a period of little work, lots of food, singing and card games, some muttered darkly about losing sight of what Christmas was really all about. There were complaints about profiteering among orange sellers, who were putting their prices up at Christmas. There was also the lawlessness, perceived or otherwise, and the drunkenness. William Prynne, a lawyer and religious puritan, echoed the thoughts of a small, but increasingly vocal, minority when he wrote that, based on the way the season was celebrated, the Saviour might be thought of as 'a glutton, an epicure, a wine-bibber, a devil, a friend of publicans and sinners'.[8]

Boars' heads and pigs in blankets: the mighty pig

I n the last few years Britain seems to have gone a bit pig crazy at Christmas, or rather pigs-in-blankets crazy. Not content with the things themselves, it's possible for the (un?) discerning would-be eater to buy pigs-in-blanket crisps, pizza, soups and ice cream. Pig is big – but also nothing new. Sausages, chipolatas and stuffing are established favourites, and while ham remains a minority choice for Christmas Day, a boiled or baked gammon looms large in many people's Boxing Day meals.

Pork has a very long connection with Christmas. Pigs are easy to rear and very versatile, hence the saying that everything can be eaten but the squeak. For those who couldn't afford poultry, or didn't have access to game, or more prestigious butchers' meats, pork was a staple. As bacon, ham and sausage meat, it was included within many other dishes habitually served as festive staples, but there were also porcine creations with a more specific association with Christmas.

The boar's head was one of the most prestigious dishes of the Christmas table from the late medieval period onwards. It even had its own carol, the first two verses of which tell you much about its presentation at the time:

The boar's head in hand bring I,
Bedeck'd with bays and rosemary.
I pray you, my masters, be merry
Quot estis in convivio [as many are as in the feast]
Caput apri defero [The boar's head I bear]
Reddens laudes Domino [Giving praises to the Lord]
The boar's head, as I understand,
Is the rarest dish in all this land,
Which thus bedeck'd with a gay garland
Let us *servire cantico*. [Let us serve it with a song]

A good boar's head was time-consuming, fiddly and expensive to prepare. It carried an air of rampant masculinity with it, for boar hunts were notoriously dangerous and exciting. Once dead, the carcass needed beheading (the head cut a way back down the spine to allow for it to be sewn together when stuffed), and then debristling, itself no mean feat. (The easiest way is to blanch and then scrape hard, before burning off the stubble, but it takes a long time and a lot of muscle.) Then it would be brined, stuffed with meat from the rest of the boar and made into a rich and heady stuffing, before being sewn up and poached for several hours. Then it was left to cool, before being decorated with gold leaf or colouring and greenery such as rosemary – not just as garlands, but stuffed in the ears, which, personal experience suggests, had the added advantage of keeping them perky if they'd flopped a bit in cooking.

Boars were extinct in England by the seventeenth century, though, and attempts to reintroduce them were never particularly successful. Instead, pigs' heads were used to replicate the effect. They are much easier to process than boars' (softer skin, smaller and less hairy), but tend to look rather less fierce and looming, erring, at times, towards almost comically piggy. Writing in the 1890s, Theodore Garrett was decidedly sniffy about their use: 'In this country wild boars are a thing of the past, and the tame boar is deemed an acceptable substitute, contributing its head with much pomp, ceremony, and fictitious admiration to the flattering guests. His paler face is duly blackened with soot and fat, to give him the ferocious aspect of an uncivilised native; but the slaughter of the innocent tame sucking pig may be considered to have reduced the wild boar and its dangerous hunting to an absurdly low ebb.'[9]

Various means were employed to tart them up, most rather more delectable than soot. They could be coated with port jelly and decorated with aspic shapes and flowers, or have sugar paste decoration applied (it had a tendency to run, as well as look 'vulgar and gaudy' according to one author).[10] Then there were the fantastical presentations illustrated in John Kirkland's *Modern Baker, Confectioner & Caterer* in

1909.[11] The ears were still stuffed with greenery, and the pigs were still just about recognisable as pigs (mainly because the eyes and nostrils have been piped round with lard). But the large surface area has become a canvas for pastry designs, which range from scenes of deer larking about to 'Best Wishes' emblazoned across the forehead. In contrast, Queen Victoria stuck to an actual boar, sent from Germany every year, which in photographs looks rather lopsided and bare versus the wild extravagances made possible with a piping bag full of pig fat.

As amazing as frolicking woodland creatures on a cold pig's head sound, some writers pushed it even further. Charles Francatelli's 1860s cake replica of a stuffed boar's head was intended to sit upon the sideboard once the real thing had been removed. It was the embodiment of playfulness, art, money and skill. The recipe starts simply, just sculpted sponge cake(s), stuck together with jam and covered with redcurrant jelly and 'transparent chocolate icing'. But it builds. The ears are pastillage, the mouth 'hollowed out and coloured of a deep scarlet inside with royal icing'. The eyes, made of gum paste dipped in sugar boiled to exactly the consistency to coat them and shine, have painted detail, and the whole is garnished, as was common with the real thing, with silver skewers stuck with what looked like cockscombs, truffles and fruits, all made from marzipan. It was to be placed upon a stand made from confectioner's paste (flour, sugar, egg, water – only theoretically edible), and, just before serving, filled with pink and white ice cream and surrounded with jelly cubes to look like aspic.[12] To give Francatelli his due, it does look utterly fantastic.

Boar also formed the basis of another standard Christmas dish, brawn. In the medieval era brawn simply meant meat, usually that of a wild boar, before it changed to denote both physical strength and a specific dish made from boar. Early recipes for brawn instruct the cook to take a vertical slice from the boar, encompassing both back and belly. It is soaked, poached with spices, rolled and tied with bands (collared) and then brined, before being sliced and served cold with mustard – or, more rarely, hot, with an orange sauce. Brawns like this were, like the boar's head, prestige dishes, and garnishing instructions tend to be lengthy and colourful. Robert May gave his garnishing instructions as a separate recipe, and suggested rosemary sprigs dipped in whipped egg white, red and yellow jelly cut into shapes, gilded bay leaves, beetroot and pickled gooseberries.[13]

Again, as boar became harder to come by, domesticated pig came to be a substitute, and brawn became a dish of, first collared, and then jellied, pork. By the eighteenth century 'mock' brawn was in vogue, made by simmering a pig's head and trotters until the flesh fell off, and pressing this meat into a dish to set: a sort of very rich and piggy terrine. In the United States this became known as head cheese (in France, too, such preparations are *fromage de tête*). Highly popular both as a commercial preparation and as something to make at home as a cheap and satisfying dish, it is still sold by some butchers today.

However, heads tend to induce squeamishness; somewhat ironic, given the popularity of sausages as another way of getting pig into Christmas dinners, and which have a long history of suspicion attached to them. The Victorians whispered of stray dogs and cats, concealed in layers of rusk and cheap pepper, while the perennial favourite, hidden horse-meat, was proven to be not such an urban legend with the horsemeat adulteration scandal in Europe in 2013.[14] Yet strings of sausages surrounded Dickens' Ghost of Christmas Past, and for those without staff they were an easy way to garnish dishes which in wealthier houses would be laden with carefully crafted stuffing balls. By the 1930s authors including Elizabeth Craig were suggesting grilled chipolatas and rolled-up rashers of bacon (cooked separately) as good for serving with Christmas poultry.

This brings us neatly back to pigs in blankets. In Britain pigs in blankets are cocktail sausages wrapped in streaky bacon, generally baked to a crisp and served as a side or a snack. They are meatier cousins of angels on horseback (oysters in bacon) and devils on horseback (prunes in bacon), both of which date to the late nineteenth century, when they were served as after-dinner savouries. As a concept, sausage-meat balls wrapped in bacon dates to the late nineteenth century. Mary Fairclough's 1911 *Ideal Cookery Book* suggested they made an excellent breakfast, luncheon or supper dish.[15] But she called them sausage cakes. Pigs in blankets did exist as a name – but not in the UK, and not for sausages in bacon. It was used in America for what the British called angels on horseback. Confused? It gets worse. By the 1930s the name, still in use in America and not the UK, sometimes meant 'titbits rolled in bacon', but could also mean 'ice-box rolls with roasted wieners' (boringly, just white rolls with baked frankfurters). This latter meaning was the one which stuck.[16] Betty Crocker popularised it in 1957, with a recipe for frankfurters rolled in ready-made dough.

At some point just after the war, the name crossed the Atlantic, but instead of becoming another term for what were, in effect, sausage rolls, became attached to things with sausage meat and bacon. Marguerite Patten's 1960 version (in a section on television snacks and sandwiches) stuffed the – full size – sausage through a roast or baked potato before wrapping the potato in bacon. She also published a hybrid recipe for lamb in blankets: lamb and bacon cubes on skewers, grilled and de-skewered into a bread roll. By the 1980s the concept of sausages – now cocktail, not full-size – wrapped in bacon had become a Christmas one. *Good Housekeeping* called them bacon rolls and specified that they were trimming for the turkey.[17] Thus, concept, name and occasion were all there: they just needed to come together, finally exploding into popular consciousness some time in the 1990s and growing ever since.

BRAWN

Hannah Woolley, 1670, *The Queen-like Closet*[18]

Brawn was originally based on boar flesh. Recipes vary wildly, but at their most basic they all involve a slab of meat which is rolled, boiled and brined. There were multiple recipes and various tips given on when and how best to prepare it. Most were stuffed, initially with spices such as ginger and mace, and later with herbs. Brines (the 'souce') were of beer or wine, and again, there's a progression from early brawns, where the brine tends to be very salty, and intended for preservation, to later souces which are more for flavour. By the seventeenth century, it was often made with pig, as boar was extinct in Britain, and by the eighteenth, 'mock brawn' was taking over – just the head of a pig, boiled until ragged, and pressed into a mould. If you buy brawn today, that's what you will get. However, the earlier version is fun to make, if a little time- (and space-) consuming. The original recipe here is sparse. I've tweaked it with elements from other contemporary sources.[19]

Original recipe:
To make a Collar of Brawn of a Brest of Pork.
Take a large Breast of Pork, and bone it, then roule it up; and tie it hard with a Tape, then boil it in water and Salt till it be very tender, then make Souce drink for it with small Beer, Water and Salt, and keep it in it: Serve it to the Table with a Rosemary Branch in the middle of it, and eat it with Mustard.

Serves 15–20

A 3kg/6lb joint of pig, skin on, cut vertically from top to
    bottom

10 whole cloves

2 blades of mace

4 bay leaves

2 litres beer (not too hoppy)

For the stuffing

3 tbsp roughly chopped sage leaves

1 tbsp roughly chopped rosemary

1 tbsp thyme

1 tbsp coarse salt

2 tsp ground ginger

½ tsp ground nutmeg

Pinch of ground mace

Pinch of ground cloves

To serve (all optional – use your imagination)

Rosemary sprigs

Bay leaves

Barberries (or cranberries)

Orange and lemon slices

Caperberries, olives or pickled plums

Gold leaf

Put the meat into a large container with enough water to cover
it and soak for 1–2 days, changing the water at least twice.

Mix the stuffing ingredients together. Open out the meat and spread with the stuffing. Roll it up very tightly and tie in place with thick cotton binding tape. Put it into a large pan with enough water to cover it, add the whole cloves, mace and bay leaves, and bring to the boil, skimming off any scum that rises to the surface. Simmer for 5 or so hours. Lots of contemporary recipes instruct the cook to 'let it boil untill it be so tender that you may thrust a straw through it', so by all means test for doneness by doing just that.[20]

Leave the meat in the pan until cool enough to handle. Remove and retie the binding, if necessary, to ensure the roll stays tight. You could also slide it into an old shirt sleeve or wrap it in cloth to keep the shape. Put the brawn into a suitable container, and strain the boiling liquid. Mix 2 litres/3½ pints of this with 2 litres/3½ pints of beer and pour it on top. Leave for at least 3 days, or up to a week.

To present, slice the brawn into thick slices, and arrange on a large plate, forming a low cone. Decorate symmetrically, using orange and lemon slices around the plate edges, a sprig or three of rosemary in the middle, and bay leaves and berries dotted artfully around. Gold leaf is optional, but it does give extra aristocratic bling. You can also fry the slices.

Serve with plenty of salt, mustard or, if hot, a sauce of 'Orange, Pepper, Gravy and beaten Butter'.

Minced meat and fruity pies

Mince pies, like so many of the foods we reserve only for Christmas, can be divisive. Mince pie haters, when pressed, tend to claim the sweetness of the filling puts them off, or that it is shop-bought pies they object to, with their oddly pale, flaccid pastry, and overly liquid interior. Others dislike all dried fruit, and regard mince pies in the same light as plum pudding or fruit cake. For those not brought up with mince pies, the term itself risks confusion. Notoriously, in 2019, the American food website The Spruce Eats published a recipe for a 'classic British Christmas treat': a mincemeat and apple tart whose developers had used minced beef as the base. The howls of laughter could be heard across the Atlantic, and the recipe was amended. However, as several commenters pointed out at the time, it wasn't that outré: the original mincemeats were, indeed, based on minced meat.

The word mince was in use as a culinary term by the

fourteenth century, applied to anything which needed to be cut up into very fine pieces. Medieval cuisine for the wealthy included a variety of dishes based on heady, sweet–savoury flavours, mixing meat with fruit, dried or otherwise, along with spice and sugar – which was treated as a spice, for it was very expensive and used sparingly. Such pies were, inevitably, served at celebration meals, as well as being very useful for giving as gifts. They were tasty, but also very impressive. Fourteenth-century chefs might make castelettes, pastry towers filled with different fillings: by the sixteenth century some diners were presented with scale models of the most modern fortifications, complete with miniature cannon firing turnip balls.[21]

By the late Tudor era minced-meat pies of this type were increasingly associated with Christmas. They were known, variously, as Christmas pies (though this term also seems to have been applied to vast, game-filled glories, which eventually took over the name completely), shred pies and, by the early seventeenth century, minced pies. Thomas Tusser listed them, as shred pies, in a 1573 ode to Christmas hospitality:

Good husband & huswyfe, now chiefly be glad,
things ha'dsom to have, as they ought to be had
They both do provide, against Christmas do come
to welcom their neighbour, good chere to have som
Good bread & good drinke, a good fyer in the hall,
brawne pudding & souse & good mustarde withal.
Biefe, mutton, & porke, shred pyes of the best,

pig, veale, goose & capon, & Turkey wel drest:
Chese, apples & nuttes, jollie Caroles to here,
as then, in the cuntrey, is counted good chere.[22]

Tusser's shred pie would have been one large pie, probably round or oval, and covered entirely with a decorated
pastry lid. While the standard pie contained veal, beef or
mutton, recipes abounded for almost any filling imaginable.
Hannah Woolley suggested a pie of calves' 'chaldrons or
muggets' (intestines) with suet, bacon, hard-boiled egg yolks,
veal, mutton and lamb, spices, onion, lemon peel and orange
juice. As was customary with a lot of pies of the time, a
caudle (sauce) of white wine and butter was to be poured in
through the airhole in the lid towards the end of cooking.
Derived loosely from earlier fast-day recipes, she also
included an egg mince pie (hard-boiled eggs, cinnamon, currants, caraway, sugar, dates, lemon peel, verjuice, rose water,
butter and salt). Other authors published recipes based on
pickled herring, salmon, eel and sturgeon.[23] Where amounts
are given, the meat to fruit ratio tends to be around 50:50
(including suet). The resulting pies are sturdy, solid, and
might just convert those who think mince pies are too sweet
or hate candied peel.

By the beginning of the eighteenth century published
recipe books sometimes included pictures along with written
descriptions. Robert May's *Accomplisht Cook* (1660) had
several illustrations of pies, including mince pies, and
later books also showed the shapes to aspire to. Although

later authors, mainly nineteenth-century folklorists, gravely advised that pies were shaped like cribs, these pictures show clearly that this is not true: it seems to have come from a few, largely satirical references, plus the determination of some Victorians to link everything Christmassy to the religious observance they thought so sorely lacking in the average celebratory knees-up.[24] Pies were intricately shaped affairs, hand-raised (moulded), in geometrical shapes which echoed those of the parterre gardens also so popular at the time. They were now individual pies, designed to be displayed together, their shapes interlinking on a large plate.

The meat in mince pies dwindled throughout the eighteenth century. They also got smaller, as cheap tin cutters and trays for tarts came on the market. Tongue continued to be popular, but tripe and calf's foot were also common meats. By the Victorian era, when the individual round mince pie was the standard form, the ratio of meat to fruit had dropped significantly. Recipes still tended to assume the cook was making enough for an entire winter season full of very keen pie-eaters, though. Eliza Acton's basic mincemeat makes around 15kg (2½ stone), of which a mere 450g (1lb) is beef. Increasingly a distinction was made between mincemeats for the rich, now using steak, and for the poor, which still used feet or other offal. Meanwhile, meat-free versions were surging back, no longer reliant on eggs, but much more likely to be a fairly standard recipe without the meat. Acton included a 'superlative mincemeat' (she wasn't wrong) which started with four large lemons, boiled until soft and minced along with their weight in apples, raisins, currants, candied peel, suet and a quarter of their weight in sugar. However, she did admit that the weight of one lemon in meat was an improvement.

The crucial era for the absolute decline in meaty mince-meats was the last quarter of the nineteenth century. In 1887, the upmarket *Encyclopaedia of Practical Cookery* listed sixteen mincemeats, nine of which included meat – around the same proportion as the more middle-class 1888 edition of *Beeton's Book of Household Management*, which has five recipes, of which three are meatless. Beeton even included a 'vegetarian mincemeat', which swapped the suet for butter. Both books also suggested making the pies themselves with puff pastry, which works brilliantly. A generation later, Beeton was reis-sued with six mincemeats, all but one without meat. The one with meat was, apparently, 'American'.

Even recipes which didn't include meat were still quite different from modern versions, though, notably in their lack of sugar. One 1888 recipe for 'mincemeat – made at xmas' in a manuscript book from York simply calls for 900g (2lb) each of currants, raisins and suet, 1.8kg (4lb) of apples and a glass of wine or brandy.[25]

By the twentieth century mincemeat was essentially meat-free, the beef suet the only reminder of a much heftier past. Where meaty mincemeats did still appear, it was very much as a historic throwback – 'Old English mincemeat', or 'cooked mincemeat' where 'the meat can be omitted if pre-ferred'.[26] The role of mince pies was also changing, though, from being served as part of a festive dinner, one among a number of choices of second-course dishes, to being a casual snack or light sweet for finishing a light meal. The complex spice mixtures of the centuries before were replaced with a pinch of cloves or, indeed, nothing at all.

By the mid-twentieth century mince pies were, like plum puddings, an intrinsic part of Christmas for many people. Factory-produced mincemeat had been available since the late nineteenth century, and bakers did a roaring trade selling ready-made pies. Inevitably, some cooks played fast and loose with the recipe, adding marmalade (delicious), banana (Australian, bit odd) or, in the twenty-first century, caramel, chocolate and nuts. Recipes using mincemeat proliferated, including the ever-reliable Fanny Cradock, whose suggestions included a Swiss roll, pancake and 'snowballs' (egged and breadcrumbed, deep-fried and dusted with sugar).[27] Others put it in bread and butter pudding, ice cream, trifle and cake. Purists may quibble, and, in some cases, it is undeniably true that the results are decidedly dubious, but if the long history of mincemeat proves anything, it is that nothing (except bad pastry) should be off the table.

MINCEMEAT

The recipes here, which are all taken from working manuscripts rather than published sources, show the steady march from high-meat, low-sugar mincemeat to the meat-free, lots of sugar version we know today. It is definitely worth experimenting with the older recipes: the meatiest ones pack quite a punch, while even the less meaty ones have a complex flavour and depth lacking from many mixtures of the later twentieth century and beyond. Whatever the recipe calls for, you can vary the type of meat you choose to use. Perhaps start with some roast beef offcuts or thinly sliced tongue before working your way up to heart, feet and tripe(!) The method is the same for all – chop or grate any large ingredients such as meat or apples into currant-sized pieces, and then mix everything together.

The original recipes nearly all make vast quantities – count on a small bathtub full. The most modern recipe, however, is considerably smaller – much more suited to a family eating mince pies only at Christmas, rather than a household with servants eating them all winter. All of these have been scaled down in the modernised version to make around 500g (just over 1lb), enough to fill a large jar and make one medium-sized pie or 24 small tarts. All can be used for pies as well as the more esoteric recipes for omelettes, rissoles, fritters, Swiss roll and pancakes which lurk in past recipe books.

c.1604: Elinor Fettiplace[28]

The meatiest of the recipes here, this makes a very solid pie, and it is worth packing the mincemeat down hard into your cases. Be very careful with the rose water – the amounts here are for the stuff sold in large bottles. Many of those on the market are rose oil in ethanol, which you can use – but they are very concentrated, so use just a couple of drops plus some water.

Original recipe:
Parboile your mutton, then take as much suet as meat, & mince it both small, then put mace & nutmegs & cinamon, & sugar & oringes peels, & currance & great reasins, & a little rose water, put all these to the meat, beat yo' spice & orange peels very small, & mingle yo' fruit & spice & all togither, with the meat, & so bake it, put as much currance as meat & twice so much sugar as salt, put some ginger into it, let the suet bee beef suet, for it is so much better than mutton suet.

110g/4oz poached mutton or leftover roast mutton
110g/4oz beef suet
Heaped ½ tsp each ground ginger, mace, nutmeg and
    cinnamon
110g/4oz currants
1 tbsp sugar
Zest of 1 small orange
110g/4oz raisins

1–2 tbsp rose water
½ tbsp salt

If you want to make a proper Tudor-style large pie, simply double the amounts given here and use a 20cm/8 inch spring-form cake tin. It is up to you whether you use a hot water crust or an enriched shortcrust pastry (shortcrust with a couple of egg yolks added).

c.1820: Ann Hailstone[29]

A surprisingly light mincemeat, both in colour and taste, especially if you use white sugar. It's important to chop the feet meat small, and to keep the spice levels up. A gang, as used in the original recipe, is four feet. A modern raw foot weighing around 1.2kg (2lb 12oz) will yield around 420g (15oz) meat – so you may wish to consider further uses for calf's feet meat (or make more mincemeat). The stewing liquor would originally have been saved for making jelly. If you can't source calves' feet, chicken or turkey would make a good substitute, as would veal – but any meat will work.

Original recipe:
Take a gang of calves' feet, boil them slowly in 6 quarts of water, till all the bones and grissels will come out, which must be done as soon as taken off the fire, and afore half the water is boiled away, then when cold, chop it very fine, and put in a lb of suet chopped very fine, a lb of currants, apples, sugar,

red wine or brandy, candied orange, nutmeg and other season-
ings to your taste, mix them all well together and bake it in
puff paste.

170g/6oz meat from a calf's foot, or other meat
80g/3oz suet
80g/3oz currants
80g/3oz minced apples
80g/3oz sugar (white or brown)
2–3 tbsp red wine or brandy
30g/1oz candied peel
⅛ tsp nutmeg, plus any other spice you like (e.g. cloves and
    cinnamon)

The use of puff pastry in the original recipe is typically mid-
nineteenth-century, though you can also use shortcrust for
the base and sides and puff for the top. Small pies were
common by this date, so it is up to you whether you prefer to
make one large pie or several smaller ones.

*c.*1940: Doreen Howling, née Stevens[30]

A rare mincemeat not involving suet, the butter makes this
very light. Butter-based recipes were around in the late nineteenth century, aimed at vegetarians, but this may have found
its way into Doreen's book due to issues obtaining suet
during rationing – it counted as part of the meat ration. It has
the advantage of making the mincemeat edible in its raw

state, so it is ideal for running through ice cream or blanc-mange or using in pancakes or omelettes, etc.

Original recipe:
½lb currants – ½lb raisins – ½lb sultanas – 1lb apples – ¼lb melted butter – ¼lb candied peel – ½lb demerara sugar – juice of lemon – salt.

80g/3oz currants
80g/3oz raisins
80g/3oz sultanas
170g/6oz apples
40g/1½oz melted butter
40g/1½oz candied peel
80g/3oz demerara sugar
Juice of ½ a small lemon
Pinch of salt

Shortcrust works best for making these into pies, and they also work as open tartlets (or as tartlets with a star-shaped or other partial lid). 20 minutes at 200°C/390°F will cook them.

Spice it up: gingerbread

Gingerbread biscuits, gingerbread houses, ginger cakes, *Lebkuchen*, ginger wines and candied ginger all find a warm welcome in our homes at Christmas. Along with cinnamon, cloves and allspice, ginger is one of those sweet spices which tends to spark a cry of 'Oh! Smells like Christmas.' As with so many of the foods associated with the modern Christmas, gingerbread started out as a rich person's feast food, before descending the social scale. In some forms it is still eaten widely outside Christmas, especially as a biscuit; though a poll in 2020 put ginger nuts a woeful fourteenth on the list of Britain's favourite biscuits. (Jaffa Cakes, shortbread and chocolate fingers made the top five. Broken Britain indeed.)

Ginger, as with most spices, first came to Europe as a medicinal ingredient and early gingerbreads were essentially medicines. The spice mixtures in them were not limited to ginger, but used a variety of spices, all with similar characteristics in medical theory. They were good for the stomach, excellent for chills, cured trapped wind and – always a bonus – were almost certainly an aphrodisiac (ginger was hot, and heat in the mouth must mean heat in the loins, right?). The earliest recipes for gingerbread appeared in the fifteenth century, when the spices were mixed with honey and thickened with breadcrumbs (or occasionally parsnips). The result was a thick, sticky cake, which one recipe suggested could be coloured red, cut into squares and decorated with box leaves held in place with a clove. A hundred years later this was sometimes termed 'red' gingerbread, to be set against 'white' gingerbread, which was essentially marzipan flavoured with spices.

Both types of gingerbread were initially consumed at the end of a meal, as part of the banqueting course. They were not specifically Christmas foods, although the association of gingerbread with alleviating over-indulgence means it must have made an appearance. In the seventeenth and eighteenth centuries, however, sugar, hitherto very much the province of the rich, started to decrease in price, along with its even cheaper alternative, molasses, which became known in the UK as treacle. Britain was busy colonising America and the West Indies, importing sugar cane and planting plantations. But costs were kept low by the mass enslavement of millions of Africans, transported to the Americas and treated horrifically. The use of slave labour was a barbaric practice which endured in British-administered colonies until 1833, and which Britons back home made excuses for as they enjoyed the fruits of other people's misery. New types of ginger-bread, made with treacle, flour and spice, were some of them.

By the late eighteenth century, gingerbread recipes were common in cookery books. Ginger biscuits, too, had appeared, sharing most of the key ingredients along with a tendency to emerge from the oven like bricks, and need days, if not weeks, of maturing to soften (not to stale so much as to become safer for the teeth). Maria Rundell's 1806 effort is typical, using 12oz of treacle mixed with 4oz of brown sugar, an egg, 1lb of butter and 'as much flour as will knead into a pretty stiff paste'. The spice mixture includes ground ginger, cloves, mace, allspice and nutmeg, plus whole coriander and caraway seeds, and the results are dark, rich and much more complex than the average ginger nut today.

Ginger biscuits – or biscuit-like cakes – were frequently moulded with wooden moulds which were used to impress a design on the mix, or cut into shapes. They were easily com-mercialised, and popular for both bakers and as fair food. Ginger was the cheapest spice of all the various possibilities, and in working-class gingerbreads it dominated. Both gin-gerbread 'husbands' and 'wives' were sold, especially on Valentine's Day, and a whole host of recipes were developed with strongly regional flavours. Northern areas favoured oats, long a bigger part of the northern diet than in the wheat-based south, and parkin emerged in the northern counties somewhere between the seventeenth century and the late eighteenth century when the name became established (it was also known as tharf cake, although not all tharf cakes were gingerbreads, and early versions were baked on a griddle, not in an oven).[31] Grasmere gingerbread, which started life as a rushbearing gingerbread, given to villagers who gathered rushes to strew the church floor, was almost certainly originally a parkin. Elsewhere wheaten recipes emerged, and by the Victorian era almost every area had its speciality.

One such speciality was pepper cake, which by the nineteenth century was confined largely to Yorkshire. It was described in 1894 as 'the children eat, at the present season, a kind of gingerbread, baked in large and thick cakes, or flat loaves, called Pepper Cakes. They are also usual at the birth of a child. One of these cakes is provided, and a cheese; the latter is on a large platter or dish, and the pepper cake upon it. The cutting of the Christmas cheese is done by the master of the house on Christmas Eve, and is a ceremony not to be lightly omitted. All comers to the house are invited to partake of the pepper cake and Christmas cheese.'[32]

By the late nineteenth century pepper cake was, in most cases, just another term for gingerbread, in which form it remained popular in Yorkshire until the 1930s. However, there are earlier recipes, including one in Martha Washington's manuscript recipe book, which show that it was once more widespread. It is unmistakably related to Flemish *peperkoek* and other, similarly named titbits still common in northern Europe, though their modern descendants are very different to the evolutionary dead end of the British version, which is hefty, to say the least. The pepper referred to allspice, known then as Jamaican pepper, which is present in the early recipes, but disappears from later ones as they become more generically gingerbready. Like other gingerbreads, early recipes are yeast-risen but raising agents such as pearl ash and both eggs and fat crept in during the nineteenth century.

By the 1890s the cake was a commercial product, requiring ageing and lending itself to bulk-baking. Whitby bakers, already known for Whitby gingerbread, advertised Whitby pepper cakes heavily at Christmas from at least the 1860s, not least as they were ideally suited for sending out by post (and were quite possibly made to the same recipe). They could be scored on top, but were frequently moulded. One correspondent to a local Yorkshire newspaper wrote 'in my childhood, pepper cake always had on top, in slight relief, a fine cluster of shiny grapes. This time – perhaps because of Coronation year – the cake was adorned with a rather grotesque representation of the lion and the unicorn.'[33] This was written in 1954, when it was clearly still being made commercially. However, it died out remarkably quickly: when readers of local papers wrote in requesting the recipe in the 1960s, the Q&A columns involved struggled to gain a response.

Gingerbread wasn't just a British phenomenon; indeed, its association with Christmas was positively muted compared to other northern European nations. Germany, in particular, had a strong attachment to all things gingery, and there a vast range of gingerbreads became as much a part of the festive season as mince pies and plum pudding did in the UK. For the Germanic royal family of Britain, gingerbreads therefore played a more significant role than they did for others.[34] Even before she married Albert of Saxe-Coburg-Gotha in 1840, Queen Victoria was surrounded by German customs, including gingerbreads at Christmas. In 1836, as a Princess, she gave her spaniel, Dash, 'a basin of bread and milk, three Indian-rubber balls, and two bits of gingerbread surrounded with branches of holly and candles'.[35] Quite what he did with the decoration is unrecorded. In 1838, now Queen, she had gingerbread given to her by her mother. Once Albert arrived, things were ramped up: 'In Germany the old saying that St. Nicholas appears with a rod for naughty children, & gingerbread for good ones, is constantly represented, & Arthur hearing of this begged for one. Accordingly Albert got up a St. Nicholas, most formidable he looking, in black, covered with snow, a long white beard, & red nose, – of a gigantic stature! He came in asking the Children, who were somewhat awed & alarmed, – "are you a good child", & giving them gingerbread & apples.'[36]

German gingerbread-like concoctions were known in Britain in the nineteenth century beyond the royals – the OED gives the first use of the word *Lebkuchen* in English as 1847. The recent vogue for German and Scandinavian gingerbreads is, in some ways, nothing new. Perhaps ironically, many of them are deliciously close to recipes of the past – *Pfeffernüsse* and other such cake-biscuit crossovers contain honey and are frequently aged to soften; *speculoos* and *pepparkakor* rely on a wide variety of spices, well beyond ginger, and the French *pain d'épices* contains honey, lots of different spices and (sometimes) rye flour, reflecting its own regionality. They stand in contrast to what, by the mid-twentieth century, was a bit of an anaemic British tradition. By the 1950s the dark, heavy gingerbread cakes of previous eras were out of fashion, replaced by lighter-tasting breads and biscuits. The spice mixtures had been simplified, the treacle replaced with sugar, or golden syrup, and cakes had declined in favour of shaped biscuits, ideal for making personalised tree decorations, or the nineteenth-century pastry-biscuit mash up which was used to construct gingerbread houses. Still, the association remains, and deepens; gingerbread cocktails, custard, trifle and ice cream may not be where we started, but they aren't at all a bad place to end up.

PEPPER CAKE

Anon, unpublished ms, *c.*1840[37]

There are very few recipes named as pepper cake, though many recipes for pepper cake-like things exist. The name is probably taken from the German for one of the many forms of gingerbread there – *Pfeffernüsse* is still a current term for small gingery biscuits, and variants on the theme are also found in Belgium, the Netherlands and Scandinavia. While recipes sometimes used yeast, as here, they also sometimes called for potash (pearlash), which again hints at German origins. (Pearlash is potassium carbonate, originally made by refining pot ashes, i.e. wood ash. It is also used to make soap, which sometimes becomes evident when using it in cooking, so I've replaced it with bicarb.) This recipe comes from an English manuscript book of the 1840s. It makes a very dense, solid cake, which is a knockout with cheese and keeps for ages. You can use molasses in place of the treacle, which wasn't commercialised until the 1950s, but the result, while lighter, isn't as interesting. While the allspice which gives the cake its name is present in the original, ginger isn't. I've added some, as I think it is an improvement.

Original recipe:
Four pounds of treacle, 4 ditto of flour, two ditto of currants well wash'd and dry'd, once pound of coarse sugar, one ditto butter, half a pound of candied lemon, 2 ounces of carraway seeds,

1 ounce of Jamaica pepper, a quarter of an ounce of cloves, beat fine, rub the butter well into the flour, warm the treacle and when all the spices are well beaten and mix'd, stir the treacle in then add a teaspoonful of potash dissolved in a cup of warm beer, a tablespoonful of salt, fill your tins only half full and bake in a moderate oven 3 hours or more – this quantity will make 4 nice sized loaves which will keep good for 12 months in a close tin box.

Makes one cake, approx. 16 × 11cm/6 × 4 inches
55g/2oz salted butter
225g/8oz flour
225g/8oz black treacle
1½ tsp ground allspice
1 tsp ground cloves
1 tbsp caraway seeds
1 tsp ground ginger
55g/2oz brown sugar
25g/1oz minced candied peel
Generous pinch of salt
½ tsp bicarbonate of soda
120ml/4floz beer, slightly warmed

Crumb the butter into the flour. Warm the treacle and add the spices along with the sugar, peel and salt. Add the treacle mixture to the flour. Add the bicarb to the beer, stir, and mix into the flour-treacle mixture.

Grease a baking tin or standard loaf tin and put the mixture in. Bake at 160°C/325°F for 2 hours, until a skewer comes out clean. Cool. It is best matured for at least a week, but if you can't wait that long, it is also excellent fresh. Eat with cheese and butter.

Drink and be merry

Complaints about people getting drunk at Christmas are as old as the celebration itself. Seizing the opportunity to get utterly plastered with the happy excuse that it is part of the festive season is a strong tradition which shows little sign of abating. But there are few specific ways of doing it. There are certainly associated drinks which most people rarely drink outside December, but they are far from universal, and most remain winter drinks, or celebratory drinks, rather than uniquely Christmas drinks.

One of the few drinks which does have a claim to be Christmassy is wassail. The word, which comes from Norse, was first recorded in the thirteenth century, as a drinking salutation, the equivalent of 'cheers'. In Middle English custom the call of 'wassail' evoked a reply of 'drink-hail'. The term quickly came into use for the drink itself, which gradually morphed from a ceremonial drink at any number of courtly occasions to something with a wider social spread, and which was associated with encouraging fruit harvests through toasting the trees, and more general carousing at New Year and Christmas. No early recipes exist, and it's clear from the many references to it that it could be any one of a number of things, but was generally based on the dominant alcoholic drink of the area.

In counties such as Kent and Herefordshire, centres of the apple-growing industry, it used cider. Elsewhere it was based on beer. In 1677 one dictionary defined wassail both as a greeting – 'be in health' and, as a wassail-bowl, as 'Spiced Ale, on New-Years Eve'. Another stated wassail was a Twelfth Night custom, 'of going about with a great bowl of Ale, drinking of healths'.[38] It was almost certainly served cold, not least as anyone going about with a great bowl full of liquid in the decidedly colder climes of the seventeenth-century Little Ice Age would rapidly find it was chilled, no matter what temperature it started at.

The first known wassail recipes are from the Georgian era, when it was also known as swig, and was served in huge, decorative bowls. One, much plagiarised, version consisted of 5 pints (2.8 litres) of beer, 4 glasses of sherry, at least half a pound (225g) of sugar, nutmeg, ginger and lemon. The recipe also instructs that 'three or four slices of bread cut thin and toasted brown' should be put into it. It was bottled and left to stand for several days, by which time it would be slightly effervescent.[39] Bread wasn't the only addition. Another variant, which also went by the name of lamb's wool, swapped the bread for roasted apples.

Wassail, then, was many things to many people. In many ways it was more of a concept than a specific thing, and the genuine traditions underlying it were starting to be lost. In 1801 one newspaper wrote of the 'curious custom' of lighting fires and drinking wassail in Herefordshire, while also noting that 'there was formerly a custom in Gloucestershire, called wassailing, or going about from house to house and Christmas or New Year's Eve, with a bowl filled with toast and ale or cyder'.[40]

As literacy increased, books grew cheaper, and recipes were codified in print, the various versions of wassail became more separate. By the eighteenth century, drinks that were at least wassail-like (though weren't wassail as such) were also being served hot. Recipes for mulled wine and ale, often with eggs added to resemble a thin custard, hit the highly desirable sweet spot between tasty, luxurious and healthy (because of the spice). Then there was bishop, later smoking bishop, which used roasted lemons or oranges studded with spice, added to hot port (and sometimes set on fire). Less genteel, but more fun, was flip, which was more of a roistering drink, a heady mix of beer and (usually) brandy, heated by dint of plunging a hot poker in it. The risk of a mouthful of soot was alleviated by the introduction of the flip-iron by the early nineteenth century, which was essentially a clean poker, kept aside for the purpose of heating the drink. By then it was also possible to buy ale or wine mullers, which took the form of a copper cone on a handle, or were sometimes boot shaped (and known as beer slippers).

By the end of the century wassail itself really was dying, though mentions of it in print were conversely increasing. It became one of those nostalgic traditions the Victorians liked to write about and try to reinvigorate. Late nineteenth-century recipes for wassail proliferated, but generally followed the pattern of beer, sherry and bread, or beer and roasted apples. By the twentieth century it was a folksy after-thought, although sporadic attempts to revive the concept in the twenty-first century have had more success. Based exclusively on the harvest-based wassail tradition, and imbued with a mish-mash of myth and romanticism, there's a fitting return to the idea (if not the reality) of regional customs in local events which involve everything from Morris dancing to toasting the urban bees of Walthamstow.

Wassail itself was abandoned by the mid-twentieth century (modern wassail events centre on mulled cider, never a sherry-boosted beer in sight). It's been replaced as a Christmas drink by port and mulled wine, with the occasional gingery cocktail. More recently, they've been joined by eggnog, itself a derivation of all those eighteenth-century, egg-thickened spiced wines, and hot toddies, whose spurious health claims and genuine gutsy glow would equally have been recognised by enthusiastic drinkers of the past.

WINE CHOCOLATE

John Nott, 1723, *The Cook's and Confectioner's Dictionary*[41]

As with so many recipes we now associate with Christmas, this would merely have been a rather lovely drink, suitable for parties, in the eighteenth century. Port was cheap, and widely consumed, with and after meals, as well as simply throughout the day, and while chocolate and sugar remained expensive, this would not have been out of the reach of the middle classes at the time. It is incredibly rich, and in a modern context would work very well as an alternative to a sweet after Christmas dinner itself, or as a somewhat unusual winter warmer to kick off a party.

Original recipe:
Take a pint of sherry, or a pint and a half of red port, four ounces and a half of chocolate, six ounces of fine sugar, and half an ounce of white starch, or fine flour; mix, dissolve, and boil all these as before. But, if your chocolate be with sugar, take double the quantity of chocolate, and half the quantity of sugar, and so in all.

Makes 750ml / 1½ pints (serves 8)
750ml / 1½ pints (1 bottle) ruby port
1 tbsp rice flour
125g / 4½oz chocolate, 70–75% cocoa solids

Mix 3 tablespoons of cold port with the rice flour to form a paste, before mixing this with the rest of the port in a pan on the hob. Heat gently. Chop or grate the chocolate and stir it in. Bring all to a very low simmer, stirring well or whisking to mix. The chocolate is ready when it is the consistency of double cream. Best served in small cups and drunk while still hot.

A BILL OF FARE FOR CHRISTMAS DAY, AND HOW TO SET THE MEAT IN ORDER (1660)

Robert May, *The Accomplisht Cook*[42]

Oysters
1 A collar of brawn.
2 Stewed broth of mutton marrow bones.
3 A grand sallet.
4 A pottage of caponets [small capons].
5 A breast of veal in stoffado
[steeped in wine with garlic].
6 A boild Partridge.
7 A chine of beef, or surloin roste.
8 Minced pies.
9 A jegote of mutton with anchove sauce.
10 A made dish of sweetbread.
11 A swan roste.
12 A pasty of venison.
13 A kid with a pudding in his Belly.
14 A steak pie.
15 A hanch of venison rosted.
16 A turkey roste and stuck with cloves.
17 A made dish of chickens in puff-paste.
18 Two bran geese rosted, one larded.
19 Two large capons, one larded.
20 A custard.

The second course for the same Mess.

Oranges and Lemons.

1 A young lamb or kid.

2 Two couple of rabbits, two larded.

3 A pig soust with tongues.

4 Three ducks, one larded.

5 Three pheasants, 1 larded.

6 A swan pie.

7 Three brace of partridge, three larded.

8 Made dish in puff-paste.

9 Bolonia sausage, and anchove, mushrooms, and caviare, and pickled oysters in a dish.

10 Six teels, three larded.

11 A gammon of Westfalia bacon.

12 Ten plovers, five larded.

13 A quince pie, or warden pie.

14 Six woodcocks, 3 larded.

15 A standing tart in puff paste, preserved fruits, pippins, &c.

16 A dish of larks.

17 Six dried neats [calves'] tongues.

18 Sturgeon.

19 Powdered [salted] geese.

Jellyes.

Cromwell's Christmas: no, he didn't ban mince pies

The seventeenth century was a pivotal period in British history. In 1649, after seven years of bitter and bloody war, crowds gathered in Whitehall to watch as Charles I, clad in two shirts so that he would not shiver in the cold and be thought a coward, was led to a scaffold and beheaded. At the time it was an almost unthinkable event, and the Civil War and Interregnum which followed left a deep and lasting mark across British society, including the way in which it celebrated Christmas.

The Puritan revolution sought to establish a new utopia, based on often radical religious and social ideals. Christmas was a problem, because of its reputation for pretty much every irreligious and anti-social activity that could be imagined. Complaints abounded. Writing in the 1580s, Phillip Stubbes stated the case clearly: '*Is it not Christmas? Must we not be merry? Truth it is: we ought both then, and at all times*

besides to be more merry in the Lord, but not otherwise, not to swill and gull more that time than at any other time ... notwithstanding, who is ignorant, that more mischief is at that time committed than in all the year besides, what masking and mumming, whereby robbery, whoredom, murder and what not is committed? What dicing and carding, what eating and drinking, what banqueting and feasting is then used in all the year besides? to the great dishonour of God and impoverishing of the realm.'[43]
The Puritans believed, not unfairly, that the pragmatism of the early church in bolting the Christian calendar on to existing festivals had left a residue of paganism around proceedings. They saw no justification for twelve days of hedonism in the teachings of the Bible, and just to add extra, if inconsistent, piquancy, argued that such wild celebration was also papist.

The general idea that Christmas tended toward riots and licentiousness wasn't that extreme. But the puritans took it too far, and by attacking Christmas in lurid terms, allowed their opponents to portray them as fun-hating authoritarians, frothing at the mouth in their desire to deny ordinary people a time of respite. Furthermore, Christmas was already seen by many as peculiarly English, and its proponents argued that, far from being a strike against the last vestiges of paganism and/or Rome, this was nothing other than a desire to undermine good old England and all it stood for. The new regime tried to avoid a direct confrontation, but in 1644 Christmas Day fell on a Wednesday – a fast day – and, under pressure from the Presbyterian Scottish, whose support the

English regime badly needed, Parliament ordered that the 25th should be kept as a fast day. The Scots had a long history of anti-Christmas legislation, starting with the Glasgow Kirk excommunicating anyone who observed it in 1583, and culminating in making its celebration illegal in 1640.

In the years following the initial legislation, new rules came in. While other festivals were all affected, the dialogue, which became increasingly vitriolic, centred on Christmas. The puritan government never explicitly banned Christmas, they simply outlawed any official celebration. And, of course, some individuals, including law-enforcers, interpreted things in their own way. Officials tore down the evergreens outside several London churches, the wardens of which were then prosecuted. In several towns there were riots in response, and people were killed as mobs forced closed the shutters on shops, and played football in the streets in flagrant breach of every law they could find. Pamphleteers on both sides enthusiastically waded into the fray, waging a war of words which gives a vivid snapshot of the way Christmas was kept. Much of the dialogue focused on material things, the stuff that people would understand and get angry about. With censorship laws abandoned, everything was up for grabs, and illiteracy was no bar – hastily produced pamphlets were designed to be read – loudly. When it came to Christmas, food was central, focusing the attention either on now-forbidden feasting and fun or, depending on your viewpoint, immorality and corruption.

Probably the most important of the foods associated with Christmas was mince pies. They really upset some writers:

Christ-mass? give me my beads: the word implies
A plot, by its ingredients, beef and pyes.
The cloyster'd steaks with salt and pepper lye
Like Nunnes with patches in a monastrie.
Prophaneness in a conclave? Nay, much more,
Idolatrie in crust! Babylon's whore
Rak'd from the grave, and bak'd by hanches, then
Serv'd up in Coffins to unholy men;
Defil'd, with superstition, like the Gentiles
Of old, that worship'd onions, roots, and lentils![44]

Little of the vitriol came directly from the pens of the puritans themselves, but instead was reported by others, with a certain amount of exaggeration. Writing in 1652, John Taylor laid into *'some over curious, hot zealous Brethren, who with a superbian predominance did doe what they could to keep Christmas day out of England'*. Apparently they *'were of opinions that ... Plumb-Pottage was mere Popery, that a Collar of Brawn was an abomination, that Roast Beef was Antichristian, that Mince Pies were Reliques of the Whore of Babylon, and a Goose, a Turkey, or a Capon, were marks of the Beast'*. Strong stuff, but a very useful list of the other foods deemed an essential part of the festive season at the time.

It is mainly due to the defenders of Christmas that the myth that the puritans actively banned mince pies or plum pudding (or, more accurately, its contemporary equivalent, plum pottage) came about. How better to inflame passion than to suggest that soldiers with swords would invade your home in search of illicit goose? Rumour ran rife that '*they assum'd to themselvs spirituall and temporall jurisdiction, power, and authority to search and plunder Pottage-pots, to ran sack and rifle Ovens, and to strip spits stark naked, and triumphantly carry the pillage to be disposed of as they pleased*'.[45] The less provocative reality was that the attempts to stop the public celebration of Christmas simply meant it moved into the private sphere. Most people carried on as they always had, focusing on their feasts behind closed doors, and while the riots grabbed headlines, they were never majority movements any more than the extremists legislating against Christmas were. The authorities wisely didn't interfere in the goings-on in private homes, except for some in London, and in return most kept their festivities out of the public gaze.

There were exceptions, though. The diarist (and then-unpublished recipe writer) John Evelyn was arrested on December 25th 1657. He'd successfully found a service to attend, only to have it invaded by soldiers as the sermon ended. 'As we went up to receive the Sacrament, the miscreants held their muskets against us, as if they would have shot us at the altar.' He spent the night under guard, but still managed to dine with a collection of titled ladies 'and some others of quality', getting home late the next day.[46]

Christmas dinners, therefore, were not drastically different to what had gone before – except in the very important respect that twelve full days of eating and drinking were hard to maintain with any degree of subtlety. They'd long been declining, though, amid occasional laments as to how good old seasonal hospitality was on the wane. The idea that wealthy landowners had once opened their doors to all was already taking hold, but it was misplaced, for all those huge medieval and Tudor feasts were based on reciprocity and the maintenance of specific relations, not encouraging random strangers to eat your carefully fattened flocks. Large-scale feasts did decline, but it was more gradual than those who later liked to blame Cromwell would admit.

Christmas Day itself remained important, along with New Year, Boxing Day and Twelfth Night, and those who could afford it still regarded the whole period as a joyous one. But there was less emphasis on particular saints and their specific days, which really did have a whiff of Catholicism about it, and, ironically in view of what the puritans were trying to achieve, more of a feeling of general, rather than religiously specific, merriment. In 1655 Brian Duppa, Bishop of Salisbury and one of very few Anglican bishops to remain in office under Cromwell, commented that 'though the religious part of this holy time is laid aside, yet the eating part is observed by the holiest of the brethren'.[47] All the battles over mince pies and plum pottage had helped to define what Christmas foods were too, and while they were very different to the forms in which we consume them today, the roots of some of our modern festive foods were now remarkably entrenched.

The monarchy was restored in 1660, and with it the recognition of Christmas as a beloved public festival. But it would never be quite the same again. Britain was openly a society of many different religious beliefs, falling broadly under the banner of Protestantism, and, while tensions remained deep and often bitterly divisive, the state did not officially persecute religious dissenters (much). A small, but determined, minority showed their disdain for Christmas by opening their shops and publishing books on Christmas Day, and it remained an issue which was guaranteed to attract attention. 'Christmas scarcely should we know, did not the almanacks it show,' declared *Poor Robin's Almanack* in 1709, and some churches complained that they were empty now on Christmas Day as people stayed away or travelled to see friends and family. Though the decline can be over-stated, it does seem as though, once the initial fever had died down, Christmas was quietly forgotten about except when it was actually happening.

FRUMENTY (FURMENTY)

Robert May, 1660, *The Accomplisht Cook*[48]

Frumenty is one of many recipes which first appeared in print as an aristocratic dish and ended up as regional working-class fare. This is a pretty typical frumenty recipe of the seventeenth century, when printed books aimed at the upper class. The spices add a refined air, making it very far removed from the purely peasant food it would come to be labelled as by later writers. By the nineteenth century it had become largely confined to Yorkshire, and was generally made with water, and sweetened with treacle. It was eaten on Christmas Eve, along with cheese and pepper cake, while the Yule log burned. Unlike other contemporary authors, May does not include currants, but they are a definite improvement. For a fast day version of it, replace the milk with almond milk, and leave out the egg. Warning: it is deceptively hefty.

Original recipe:
Take wheat and wet it, then beat it in a sack with a wash beetle, being finely hulled and cleansed from the dust and hulls, boil it over night, and let it soak on a soft fire all night; then next morning take as much as will serve the turn, put it in a pipkin, pan, or skillet, and put it a boiling in cream or milk, with mace, salt, whole cinnamon, and saffron, or yolks of eggs, boil it thick and serve it in a clean scowred dish, scrape on sugar, and trim the dish.

Serves 2, for breakfast, 4 if part of a meal
100g/4oz wheat grain, preferably quick cook (e.g. Ebly)
250ml/½ pint full-fat milk
¼ tsp ground cinnamon
Pinch of ground mace
¼ tsp saffron strands
Generous pinch of salt
25g/1oz currants
1 egg yolk
1–3 tbsp crème fraiche or double cream
Optional: brown sugar, to serve

If your wheat grain is not of the quick-cook type, follow the instructions on the packet and soak it overnight in water to tenderise, if needed. Cook it in water for around 10 minutes less than the packet suggests, until soft, but still with some bite. If you are using pre-cooked grains, there is no need for this step.

Add the grain to your milk and bring gently to a very low simmer. Cook for 5 minutes before adding the ground spices, saffron strands, salt and currants. Continue to cook until nearly all of the milk has been absorbed – about 10 minutes. Remove from the heat and stir in the egg yolk, which will cook through in the heat left in the mixture. Add the cream or crème fraiche and serve.

Sprinkling sugar on top is optional. I'd suggest tasting first, for the dish is very rich and naturally sweetened by the milk.

From plum pottage to Christmas pudding

Before Christmas pudding there was plum pudding, and before plum pudding there was plum pottage. All three share a rich, spicy set of flavours, laden with dried fruit and thickened with breadcrumbs. Two are virtually unheard of today, and the third is under threat. Twenty-first-century polls suggest that the popularity of Christmas pudding is age-related, and that the more youthful revellers among us do not fully comprehend its dark, delicious glories.

The origins of Christmas pudding lie in medieval cuisine. The food of the era included roast and boiled meats, pies, nut milk jellies and complex sweet–savoury concoctions, but one of the most basic elements was pottage. Pottages were essentially things boiled in a pot (the word is related to both porridge and potage, i.e. soup). For the poor, this usually meant pulses or grains and whatever vegetables and herbs were to hand for flavour. For the rich, pottage more often contained meat (or fish for fast days), spice, and other expensive imports such as dried fruit. The same basic recipe could be treated in lots of different ways. Frumenty, for example, could either be a hearty barley porridge, or a delicate, spiced delight (admittedly still a hearty one). At the time, plum was simply a term for dried fruits, particularly grapes, hence anything containing them gained the name 'plum'. Actual plums were strictly unnecessary.

The term plum pottage appeared in print in the 1570s, although printed recipes weren't in circulation for another hundred years or so. Robert May's 1660 version is typical: a thick soupy mixture based on a heavily reduced meat stock, plump with raisins and with a kick of spice. One nineteenth-century writer damned it as 'a savoury-sweet slop', which, it must be admitted, isn't that inaccurate.[49] Like so many foods which would later become indelibly associated with Christmas, it was first and foremost a feast food, but because it was seasonal in winter it quickly became part of the festive season: 'Plum-Porridge is good all the Year, but in Fashion at Christmas, with the Pipes, Cards, Roast-Beef, and Dice, and many a Song, and carousing Night and Day.'[50] It wasn't to everyone's taste. One bewildered eater described it as having 'fifty different tastes', while the Swiss travel writer Caesar de Saussure simply remarked that it 'is a dish few foreigners find to their taste'.[51] Yet it was extremely popular among those who could afford it, and remained widely eaten into the late eighteenth century, by which point it had co-existed with its eventual successor for around 150 years.

The eclipse of plum pottage by plum pudding was very

gradual. But even by the late eighteenth century the plum pudding was clearly in the ascendant. This 1791 poem, along with demonstrating the casual anti-French sentiment of the time, centres on the key element of the pudding cloth, by now one of the most crucial components of the eighteenth-century British *batterie de cuisine*:

To make a plum-pudding, a French Count once took
An authentic receipt, from an English Lord's cook:
Mix suet, milk, eggs, sugar, meal, fruit, and spice,
Of such number, such measure, such weight, and such price;
Drop a spoonful of brandy, to quicken the mess;
And boil it for so many hours—more or less.—

These directions were tried, but when tried had no good in;
'Twas all wash and all squash—but 'twas not English
    pudding:
And Monsieur in a pet sent a second request,
For the cook that prescrib'd, to assist when 'twas drest;
Who of course to comply with his Honour's beseeching,
Like an old cook of Colebrook, march'd into the kitchen.

The French cooks, when they saw him, talk'd loud and
    talk'd long;
They were sure all was right; he could find nothing wrong:
Till just as the mixture was rais'd to the pot,
'Hold your hands! Hold your hands!' scream'd astonish'd
    John Trot

'Don't you see you want one thing, like fools as you are?'
—'Vone ting, Sar! Vat ting, Sar!'—'A Pudding
      Cloth,—Sar!'

As an urban myth, the coming together of a perplexed cook (usually French) and an employer who took for granted that everyone knew how to make plum pudding had a long currency. Even in the twentieth century the tale was being retold, at the expense of both the ignorant cook and the bizarre British obsession with their national pudding.

There are possible mentions of puddings boiled in cloths in the medieval era, but the real heyday of the pudding was from the seventeenth century onward. Plum pudding is mentioned in text by 1630, and by the end of the seventeenth century several related puddings had also made their appearance. One of these, hackin, a northern English and Scottish borders pudding based on meat, fruit and spice, became equally associated with Christmas. Richard Bradley declared proudly in 1728 that in Lancashire and Cumberland 'it is a Custom with us every Christmas-Day in the Morning, to have, what we call an Hackin'.

Plum pudding, meanwhile, took off nationally. Early recipes contained mainly currants and raisins, plus the key ingredient of suet. Like most fats, suet is a brilliant flavour carrier, and when hot is also meltingly soft and light. When cold, it hardens, meaning that a pudding made with suet is mouth-wateringly succulent if eaten hot, but sets solid when cold. It was ideal for sending by post, or keeping at the back of a cupboard, and kept for months (years in the case of some modern puddings). It could be made and served straight away, or cooled and kept until needed, to be reheated for an hour or so and served whole – or cut into slices and fried. Like plum pottage, it was also satisfyingly weird to visitors from abroad. By the mid-eighteenth century it had joined roast beef as a symbol of Britishness, and as the satire industry boomed under George III, the likes of Gilray and Rowlandson enthusiastically seized upon it to stand in for the nation.

It was solid, plain (but with hidden depths) and it drew upon the produce of a rapidly expanding empire. Roast beef and plum pudding became as inextricably entwined as tea and milk, or bread and butter. Plum pudding was served as a side dish to the beef, the two eaten together with the pudding taking the role that chutney, Cumberland or cranberry sauce does on tables today. The two were eaten widely, well beyond Christmas, and were the staple food of grand celebrations, such as coronation feasts. But they were very much a part of Christmas, even for the poor(ish). Charles Lamb summed up the appeal, as well as the continued orthographical dilemma of the time, declaring happily that 'I always spell plumb-pudding with a b., p-l-u-m-b, I think it reads fatter and more suetty.'[52]

Satirists universally portrayed the plum pudding as can-nonball-shaped, i.e. boiled in a cloth, but they were behind the fashionable curve (their puddings are also slightly opti-mistic, for the average pudding settles into slightly more of an oval shape than most of the illustrations). Ceramic and copper culinary moulds were a large part of the late-Georgian kitchen scene, and many of the moulds mistakenly dismissed as jelly moulds by country house visitors today were intended for boiling puddings (and baking cakes). In the nineteenth century moulds decreased in price as manufacturing techniques improved, and plum puddings were often moulded. A wisely chosen mould allows for a great deal of brandy to hang about the tops and sides, meaning that when the tradition of lighting the pudding on fire made its appearance the canny cook could really make quite a spectacle.

It is to the Victorians, inevitably, that we owe many of the characteristics of the modern Christmas pudding. They weren't the first to call plum pudding a Christmas pudding – the term was used occasionally by at least the mid-eighteenth century, possibly earlier, but it didn't come into common usage until the middle of the nineteenth century. Elizabeth Hammond included a 'boiled plum, or Christmas pudding' in the 1819 edition of her *Modern Domestic Cookery*, and in 1845 Eliza Acton used both plum pudding and Christmas pudding interchangeably. (Her Author's Christmas Pudding remains one of the best recipes going, in my view.) By this point setting it alight was well established, too – one of the most famous literary plum puddings, that of Mrs Cratchit, was borne to the table 'blazing in half or half a quartern of ignited brandy'. Where the idea came from is less obvious, but the link between fire and Christmas was as old as Christmas itself, and flames make everything more fun. It also to helped differentiate Christmas pudding from plum pudding.

The mid-century also saw a rash of rather tongue-in-cheek references to 'Stir Up Sunday', the Sunday before Advent, when the Collect (official prayer) for the day starts 'Stir up, I beseech thee'. The idea of the family cosily gathering to stir the plum pudding was at odds with Victorian reality, with working-class families increasingly scattered, especially if in service, and upper-class families eating plum pudding all winter – and not exactly frequent kitchen visitors. However, it chimed with the new Christmas, as promoted by Dickens and his ilk. While it remained a minority activity, the idea took hold, until by the Edwardian period Stir-Up Sunday had become, if not heavily practised, at least widely known as a vague tradition.

By the late nineteenth century plum pudding was giving way to Christmas pudding. It was declining as a general winter dish, and becoming a one-day dish instead. By the 1890s the final piece of the modern puzzle was in place: 'some housewives put a thimble, a ring, a piece of money, and a button, which will influence the future destinies of the recipients'.[53] This custom was transported from the twelfth cake – of which, more later. Meanwhile, as service style changed, and sequential courses came in during the last quarter of the century, the newly rebranded Christmas pudding was divorced from the roast beef, and slowly slid into place as part of the second part of the meal, among the sweet dishes and lighter puddings. It never sat very happily there, and as late as 1900 Queen Victoria's Christmas menus included plum pudding with the roasts. She was eating the meal of a bygone era, though: her successors pushed it to the end, and there it remains.

In some ways the apogee of the Christmas pudding was the mid-twentieth century. It was then that many of the more outré myths around it came into being – the idea that it should contain thirteen (or twelve) ingredients to represent the apostles, or the banning of Christmas pudding by Oliver Cromwell being just a couple of the more obviously false claims. Christmas pudding fervour was very real, especially between the two world wars, fanned by both manufacturers and the government, who – understandably – saw Christmas pudding as a focal point for the British population as Christmas. It was explicitly recognised as a national symbol, and was genuinely universal across the class divides. For the food industry, it could be used to sell all sorts of products – recipes for Christmas pudding jelly appeared (generally they result in a fruity chocolate blancmange – by no means horrid), along with puddings which included everything from 'raisely' (surely one of the best-named baking powders going), to angostura bitters.[54] For the government, it proved a useful tool in promoting both national pride and international trade, mainly in the form of the 'Empire' pudding. Elaborated by Henri Cédard, head chef to George V, the original recipe would happily have served about fifty people. It was slimmed down and widely distributed, the recipe proudly proclaiming the origins of the seventeen ingredients which went into it.

Compared to pudding recipes of just fifty years before, it was darker, richer and crumblier – far more recognisable as a modern-style pudding, and destined to be served with a sweet white sauce or brandy butter.

The Empire pudding died a death, as with so many foods reliant on imported ingredients, when rationing was brought in from 1940 to 1954. Wartime cookery books determinedly gave recipes for Christmas pudding, reliant on hoarded fruit and fat, and bulked out with the ubiquitous carrot. Pale and insipid, they are a shadow of what went before, and they go mouldy remarkably fast. It is not surprising that 1950s recipes veer enthusiastically towards the luxurious and include just as many potentially ill-advised ingredients as their 1930s ancestors – though Elizabeth Craig's banana plum pudding is surprisingly tasty. As the British Christmas dinner became increasingly codified in the last half of the twentieth century, pudding remained in place, by now the most venerable foodstuff present (along with mince pies). Inevitably commercialised, shop-bought puddings took advantage of the improved keeping qualities of the newer iterations of plum pudding, and recipes increasingly called for lengthy ageing, the make-it-and-eat-it-on-the-day habits of the past forgotten.

The average Christmas dinner in the first quarter of the twenty-first century is 5,000 calories. Fat still hasn't recovered its shine from decades of demonisation based on dodgy science in the 1970s. Christmas pudding, long regarded outside Britain and British-influenced countries as a strange aberration, is losing ground. The majority of festive tables still include it, but trifle, yule log and a box of chocolates are gaining in popularity. Pudding-doubters lurk everywhere, unconvinced that it is a suitable end to an already hefty meal. Perhaps they should try it where it sat for so long, next to their roast beef, a flaming centrepiece and not a briefly spar-kling afterthought.

PLUM POTTAGE

Charles Carter, 1732, *The Compleat City and Country Cook*[55]

Recipes for plum pottage are surprisingly scarce, although many others which aren't specifically labelled as such would yield very similar results. It is very hard to fit it into modern dining patterns, as it is neither a soup nor a stew, and neither definitely savoury, nor sweet. For that reason, it is probably easiest to enjoy on its own as a historical curiosity – perhaps for a light(ish) Christmas Day supper, or a stomach-lining snack before the drinking starts. However, it also makes an excellent accompaniment to roast meat, in which form it starts to approach its true glory. I'm not averse to it spread on toast either.

Original recipe:
Take a leg of beef, boil it to rags, so that the liquor when cold will be a jelly, strain it while hot, let it stand while it is cold, take off the fat very clean, then set it over the fire again, and to every gallon of broth allow half a pound of raisins of the sun, and a pound of currants, clean pick'd and wash'd; also stew two pound of prunes, and when they are plumpt take out the fairest, and put in whole, the remainder pulp thro' a colander, wash the stones and skins clean with some broth; add the crumb of a penny white loaf grated to each gallon of your broth, and the quantity of half a nutmeg to a gallon, the weight of a nutmeg of cloves and

*mace, and the weight of all the spices of cinnamon, grate and
beat the spice fine; put in for each gallon half a pint of sack and
half a pint of claret, add salt and sugar to your palate; when the
fruit is plump it is enough: just before it is taken off the fire
squeeze in the juice of a lemon to each gallon, and put in a peel
or two.*

Makes about 600ml/1 pint (serves 4)
Approx. 750g/1½lb bone-in beef – short ribs or shin are
    ideal
110g/4oz prunes, soaked for a few hours if very dry
25g/1oz raisins
55g/2oz currants
⅛ tsp ground nutmeg
¼ tsp each ground cloves and mace
1 tsp ground cinnamon
75g/3oz white or whiteish breadcrumbs (about 3 slices,
    crusts removed)
25ml claret
25ml sherry
The juice and finely grated zest of ½ a lemon
Generous pinch of salt
2–3 tbsp brown sugar

It is worth making the basic stock the day before you plan to
serve the pottage. Simply put the beef in a large, heavy-
bottomed saucepan, add 3 litres/6 pints of water (which
should cover the meat), and bring slowly to the boil. Skim off

the scum which rises to the surface and discard. Once the liquid is boiling, reduce the heat to a simmer, put a lid on the pan and leave for around 2½ hours until, in the words of the original recipe, it is boiled 'to rags'. Remove the bones and meat (there will be no flavour in it: it is best fed to the dog), and leave the stock in a cool place overnight to cool completely.

The next day the fat should have formed solid pools on top of the stock. Skim it off and strain the stock through a jelly bag or sieve lined with muslin. Put it into a clean pan and boil fast until it is reduced to around 600ml/1 pint. This should take around 1–1½ hours.

Finely chop half the prunes, leaving the other half whole. Add all the fruit, the spice, and the breadcrumbs to the stock and heat gently until the breadcrumbs have disintegrated, acting as a thickener. Add the claret, sherry, lemon juice and zest and good pinch of salt. Heat through and taste before adding the sugar.

HACKIN

Richard Bradley, 1736, *The Country Housewife and Lady's Director*[56]

Described as 'a pudding made in the law [stomach] of a sheep or hog … formerly a standard dish at Christmas', hackin was one of the many close cousins or possible forbears of plum pudding.[57] It was apparently linked to a tradition whereby the hackin 'must be boiled by day-break, or, else, two young men must take the maiden [i.e. the cook] by the arms and run her round the market-place, till she is ashamed of her laziness'.[58] Harsh. It was regularly called 'the great sausage', presumably because it was boiled in a stomach, and is also related to haggis. It was predominantly a northern dish, and this version was originally 'from a gentleman in Cumberland'. Actual recipes are scarce, and it seems to have largely died out by the nineteenth century, swept away by the ubiquity of plum pudding. However, it makes an unusual starter, and is, as suggested by contemporary sources, excellent fried up for breakfast. It was also sometimes served as an accompaniment to roast meat, and would not be out of place as a modern stuffing. For a modern twist, it is excellent with turkey in lieu of beef and cranberries in place of the currants.

Original recipe:
Take the Bag or Paunch of a Calf, and wash it, and clean it well with Water and Salt; then take some Beef-Suet, and shred it

small, and shred some Apples, after they are pared and cored, very small. Then put in some Sugar, and some Spice beaten small, a little Lemon-Peel cut very fine, and a little Salt, and a good quantity of Grouts, or whole Oat-meal, steep'd a Night in Milk; then mix these all together, and add as many Currans pick'd clean from the Stalks, and rubb'd in a coarse Cloth; but let them not be wash'd. And when you have all ready, mix them together, and put them into the Calf's-Bag, and tie them up, and boil them till they are enough. You may, if you will, mix up with the whole, some Eggs beaten, which will help to bind it … I had forgot to say, that with the rest of the Ingredients, there should be some Lean of tender Beef minced small.

Serves 10–12 as part of a bigger meal or 6 with roast potatoes, chutney, etc.

225g/8oz beef mince (you can also use veal or pork)
110g/4oz oatmeal, soaked overnight in 200ml/7fl oz milk
1 apple, grated
110g/4oz currants
1 egg
The zest of 1 lemon
1 tsp sugar
½ tsp ground allspice
½ tsp ground mace
¼ tsp ground cinnamon
1 tsp salt
110g/4oz suet
Butter, to grease the paper

Put a pan of water on to boil. Mix all the ingredients together, ending with the suet. You should have a firm, mouldable dough. Shape this into a large sausage, approx. 25cm/10 inches long. Wrap this in greased baking parchment, and then in a wetted and floured pudding cloth, tying the ends up so it looks like a giant boiled sweet in a wrapper. Lower this carefully into the water, and maintain at a rolling boil for 3 hours. Do not let the pan boil dry.

Remove from the pan, allow to cool enough to handle (and firm up a bit) and unwrap the cloth. Carefully peel off the paper. You can serve as is, but it is infinitely better left to cool completely, then cut into slices and fried in butter or lard.

BILL OF FARE FOR DECEMBER (1791)

Richard Briggs, *The English Art of Cookery*[59]

First Course

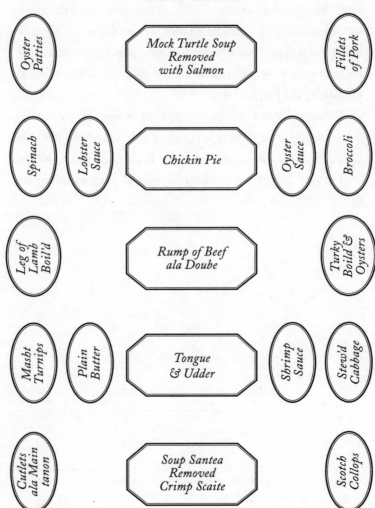

Oyster Patties

Mock Turtle Soup Removed with Salmon

Fillets of Pork

Spinach

Lobster Sauce

Chickin Pie

Oyster Sauce

Broccoli

Leg of Lamb Boil'd

Rump of Beef ala Doube

Turky Boild & Oysters

Masht Turnips

Plain Butter

Tongue & Udder

Shrimp Sauce

Stew'd Cabbage

Cutlets ala Main tanon

Soup Santea Removed Crimp Scaite

Scotch Collops

Second Course

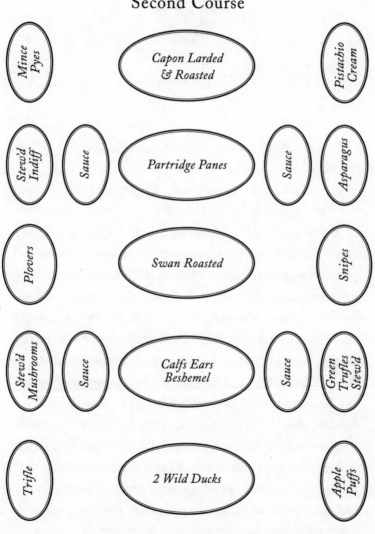

Mince Pyes

Capon Larded & Roasted

Pistachio Cream

Stew'd Indiff

Sauce

Partridge Panes

Sauce

Aspargus

Plovers

Swan Roasted

Snipes

Stew'd Mushrooms

Sauce

Calfs Ears Beshemel

Sauce

Green Trufles Stew'd

Trifle

2 Wild Ducks

Apple Puffs

Trifling things

Trifle's a controversial topic. Christmas foods do tend
toward the divisive – from descriptions of plum pudding
as 'the devil's food' to those of brandy butter as 'a sugary
cyst'.[60] But trifle really gets people going. Responses to one poll
(mine) about why it was a Christmas food included 'it is the
very pinnacle of perfection', to 'booze and cream!' But there
were also heated debates about the inclusion of alcohol, bought
cake vs home-made cake and – the ultimate trifle touch paper –
to jelly or not to jelly – and was jam an acceptable substitute, or
should all such things be banned? Trifle is by no means as tied
to Christmas as many of the other foods in this book, but it is a
constant presence in surveys of Christmas dinners. Done well,
it shares many of the characteristics of other festive foods – it is
time-consuming to make, it looks spectacular, it is expensive,
and it is best shared between a large group of people. Done
badly, it is a mess of soggy cake and overly sweet booze, a slimy
bowl of clashing flavours and terrible textures.

Trifle didn't always involve the things that make trifle-haters hate trifle. The earliest mentions of trifle as a dish date to the 1590s, and a recipe appeared in Thomas Dawson's 1596 *The Good Huswife's Jewell*. It is simply gently warmed, sweetened cream, flavoured with ginger and rose water and served in a bowl. The name derived from Middle English (and before that, French) and meant, then, as now, a thing of little importance, a whimsy, and this recipe is certainly a whimsical delight. As with so many puddings, it was part of a whole family of related dishes, not always clearly delineated, and it has variously been described as the ancestor of fools, syllabubs, set creams and blancmange.[61] However, as a recipe called trifle, its immediate future lay in a slightly different direction. By the 1670s, when trifle was making regular appearances in printed recipe books, it was more akin to junket (sweetened curds). Hannah Woolley's 1670s trifle instructs the reader to 'take sweet cream, season it with rose-water and sugar, and a little whole mace, let it boil a while, then take it off'. Rennet is then added, which will make the mixture more like curds and whey, and when it is served 'strew on some French comfits'.

Comfits were caraway or fennel seeds (among others) coated in successive layers of sugar, immensely time-consuming to prepare, and popular as breath fresheners, palette cleansers and garnishes. They were the forerunner of the hundreds and thousands so popular for trifles in the 1980s. Three hundred years of continuity – but only in decorative terms.

It wasn't until the 1750s that trifle started to become something really recognisable today. Hannah Glasse is notorious for plagiarising most of the recipes in her *Art of Cookery Made Plain and Easy*. However, with her recipe for trifle in the 1751 edition of the book she seems to have done something new, writing down (if probably not devising) the first trifle with a biscuit base soaked with fortified wine and topped with custard and cream or something like it (she used syllabub, which is lighter and nicer). In 1760 she followed this up with 'a grand trifle' in which biscuits were embedded in wine jelly, topped with sweetened cream and garnished with flavoured jams, fruit jellies and cake soaked in sherry along with syllabub. The biscuits, being ratafias (modern crisp amaretti work as well), stay crispy as long as it isn't made too far in advance, unlike many modern trifles which rely on well-soaked sponge. She specified that it should be arranged 'as high as you can possibly raise it; this is fit to go to the King's table, if well made, and very excellent when it comes to be all mixed together', which is not only indicative of its looks, but also of the enthusiasm with which diners should dig in.

Syllabub was used in a lot of early recipes. Unlike modern syllabubs, which are fairly heavy mixtures of flavoured and sweetened whipped cream, eighteenth-century 'whipt' versions are ethereal froths which disappear in the mouth. They were made with the equivalent of single cream, flavoured with wine, beer or cider, plus sugar and sometimes other flavourings, and whisked until a froth formed. This was very much not whipped cream: the froth was more like bath foam, and was usually taken off and laid on a sieve to dry out slightly before being served floating on a bed of the liquid which had drained from it. Piled on a trifle, it would have looked beautiful, adding a real delicacy to a dish which risked being rather rich and heavy. Trifle would have been just one among many sweet dishes on offer as part of the upper-class Georgian meal, sitting alongside such things as plum pudding, mince pies, fruit tarts, jellies and creams.

Once established, the new trifle was eagerly adopted. By the nineteenth century it was a British staple, although as with any dish there were other, closely related recipes including tipsy cake (a Savoy sponge soaked in alcohol and served with custard) and whim-whams (essentially another name for trifle in the eighteenth century). It was eaten, too, in British-influenced countries such as America, and colonies including New Zealand, but was rather disdained by the French, unless they'd become anglicised. Theodore Garrett called them 'Exceptionally English', but also included thirteen recipes (including a couple of savoury trifles), concluding that, despite the name, 'trifles are not by any means unimportant dishes'.[62] Recipes generally ran along vaguely similar lines, with biscuits or cake, soaked in an admirably eclectic selection of alcohol (there were also temperance trifles using fruit juice), custard, cream and jam, fruit jellies or marmalade. Garrett's Queen of Trifles (it really is) used both cake and macaroons, a thick almond custard, jam (or fruit jelly) and he threw crystallised fruit into the mixture for good measure. Others, meanwhile, advised using tinned fruit and packet custard. Already there were murmurs against the trifle, though. Alexis Soyer advised 'trifles are generally considered unwholesome; I think it is because they are often made too long before they are wanted, and because no spirit is used in the cake, the consequence is, the cream turned sour.' He also suggested dying the custard pink. If you were going to trifle, go over the top or go home.

The twentieth century is where it all went wrong for certain modern trifle-haters. Up to this point, while jelly made with gelatine was sometimes present, most recipes called for 'jam, marmalade or jelly', the inference being that they meant jelly in the sense of a fruit jelly, i.e. a clear jam, set with pectin, which was spread on the cake or cut into pieces and put on top (which is also the current sense in America). But with the advent of packet gelatine, and then ready-made cubes of jelly, plus artificial flavouring and colourings, jelly made with gelatine slid from the upper-class dinner table to nursery food. Whether through misunderstanding or desire, it also became part of trifle. In the 1950s, Constance Spry's entirely mainstream recipe called for sponge cake, sherry, brandy, strawberry or raspberry jam, custard, whipped, sweetened, vanilla-flavoured cream, plus almonds, angelica and ratafia biscuits to decorate (apparently 'in these decadent days sherry alone is generally used').[63] But by 1960 Marguerite Patten's characteristically quirky criss-cross trifle (the top is a layer of custard with a noughts and crosses game piped on) used sherry-flavoured gelatine-based jelly. Patten was aiming at a broader and less aspirational audience than

Spry, and her style of trifle was the one which would triumph. It wasn't – and isn't – universal, but a search for trifle recipes online brings up a multitude of recipes using gelatine-jelly rather than jam-jelly. Horrifically, sometimes they call for both.

The trouble is, it all gives trifle a terrible reputation. The Americans have long since forgotten it was part of their culinary repertoire, and mention of trifle now brings up only references to *Friends* (look it up) and a puzzled frown. One (admittedly tongue-in-cheek) website explains it as a 'retro, layered dessert … almost camp in its multi-colored brashness. Its bedrock is a sponge, sometimes encased in Jell-O, followed by a thick custard subsoil, whipped cream surface, and scattering of grated dark chocolate or a kitsch cherry.'[64] Closer to home, in a truly eye-opening episode of the French series *Le Meilleur Pâtissier* (the *Great British Bake Off*, version Française) in 2018 the technical challenge was a 'trifle royal'. Moulded, with no bowl in sight, it was composed of brandy and sugar-syrup-soaked Genoise sponge layers sandwiched together with jellied cream studded with strawberries, and topped with a dome of murky sugar-and-water jelly full of fruit.[65] The dome bounced. The contestants were appalled. No wonder British food gets such bad press.

It's fair to say that there are trifles, and there are trifles. It is one of those dishes which is easy to personalise, and therefore easy to love (your own) or hate (anyone else's). It also goes far beyond Christmas, although there are a few recipes which have very specific links to the season. In the 1890s

Cassell's published a recipe for 'a Christmas dish', essentially a Swiss roll trifle, made with a layer of Swiss roll, macaroons soaked in redcurrant jelly heated up with sherry, raisin wine and sugar. It was topped with thick custard and studded with almonds.[66] Fanny Cradock, a huge fan of making historic recipes accessible to modern cooks, built on this in her Christmas recipe series, adding 'plonk', chocolate chips, cream and decorating it with glacé cherries, angelica and chocolate leaves stabbed into the rim.[67] It is only a small step to using a yule log, which surely must be the ultimate, undeniably festive, trifle.

TIPSY CAKE

Eliza Acton, 1845, *Modern Cookery*[68]

As a confirmed trifle-hater, I briefly considered putting a nice, savoury trifle in here, based on lobster in a fried bread cup. But honesty compels me to admit it is more of a croustade, and a cheat's way out. If soggy, booze-imbibed cake is your thing, here is the ultimate in the genre. Tipsy cake was the early nineteenth century's build on trifle: just cake, alcohol and a token custard sauce. Those who dislike the jelly in modern trifles may well rejoice in this, therefore. The cake used was a Savoy cake, a fatless sponge made in a highly decorative and tall mould with a characteristically flat top. It gave the dish a height lacking from more sloppy trifles, served in bowls, and marked the host out as having the kind of kitchen which was stocked with copper moulds – and the kind of cook who could produce fancy sponges in slightly unpredictable ovens. Later recipes went even more over the top, reaching a sort of Tipsy Cake on hallucinogenic drugs, garnished liberally with ratafia biscuits, jam, cream, candied fruits and custard. Done in this way Tipsy Cake is jaw-dropping as a festive centrepiece. Even I have to admit that it is genuinely delicious.

Original recipe:
The old-fashioned mode of preparing this dish was to soak a light sponge or Savoy cake in as much good French brandy as it

could absorb; then, to stick it full of blanched almonds cut into whole-length spikes, and to pour a rich cold boiled custard round it. It is more usual now to pour white wine over the cake, or a mixture of wine and brandy; with this the juice of half a lemon is sometimes mixed.

Serves 10–12 (use a cake mould which holds 1.25–1.5 litres / 2–3 pints)

For the Savoy cake
Butter, plus a little flour and sugar, for lining the mould
120g/4oz flour
4 eggs
1 tsp lemon juice
160g/6oz caster sugar
The finely grated zest of 1 small lemon

To make the cake tipsy
75ml/2½fl oz white wine
150ml/5fl oz brandy (you could also use just brandy, or switch the wine and brandy for port, ginger wine, sherry, etc.)

For the custard
3 egg yolks and 1 white
25g/1oz caster sugar
Orange flower water, to taste (you can also use vanilla)
300ml/½ pint full-fat milk
Optional (but wise): 1 heaped tbsp cornflour

To decorate

Blanched almonds

Optional: whipped cream, jam, candied fruits, ratafia
   biscuits

A few days before you plan to serve your tipsy cake, make the
Savoy sponge. Start by greasing a tin. If you have a Savoy
cake mould, great! Otherwise a bundt mould would work –
or anything with a bit of height and interest. Grease it well,
making sure you get into all of the crevices, then shake a
mixture of flour and caster sugar in, shaking the tin to coat
before pouring out the excess.

Sift the flour (Acton is adamant that a great deal of sifting
is the way to a good sponge). Whisk the eggs, lemon juice
and sugar together until pale and foamy. Now fold the flour
into the egg mixture, and add the lemon zest, being careful
not to knock too much air out. Pour the batter into the prepared tin and bake for 40–45 minutes, until a skewer comes
out clean. Cool in the tin for 10 minutes before turning out on
to a wire rack. Leave the cake for around 5 days to get stale.

When you are ready to make your tipsy cake, simply place
it in a shallow dish. Pierce the cake in several places. Mix the
wine and brandy together and pour it slowly over the cake.
Leave for at least 30 minutes, then carefully pour off any
excess.

For the custard, whisk the egg yolks and white with the
sugar and orange flower water (or vanilla). Mix 3 tablespoons
of milk with the cornflour and set aside. Now heat the rest of

the milk until just below boiling, and pour on to the yolks, whisking. Mix thoroughly and add back to the pan, along with the cornflour mix (this stabilises the custard and helps to stop it curdling). Heat without boiling until the mixture thickens, then remove from the heat.

Allow the custard to cool and pour it round the bottom of your tipsy cake (any excess can be served on the side). Stick the cake with almonds 'so as to resemble a porcupine' (neatly covering the holes you made for the wine). After that, it is up to you. Adding ratafias, extra cream or candied fruits will give you visual wow as well as extra flavour and texture. Don't put the biscuits on too early, though, or they will lose all of their crisp, and there really is enough soggy cake in this already.

A nice bit of cheese

Ah, yes, the annual argument over where the cheese course should sit. Cheese is not just for Christmas – it is most definitely a year-round food. But today's Stilton makers sell around 70% of their output at Christmas, and most cheesemongers offer dedicated Christmas cheese boards for those who just can't choose.

Just as with the rest of the Christmas meal, cheese is (or should be) seasonal. Hard cheeses which require ageing, such as Stilton and its raw-milk cousin Stichelton (and Wensleydale, Cheddar and Lancashire) are at their best in the winter. Stilton was marketed from the start well beyond the region, sold largely through the Bell Inn in the village it was named after, and quickly gained a following among those travelling up or down the country. Cheeses which came in big, hard wheels were ideal for sending as gifts, especially when they were expensive, which made them ideal for Christmas.

But cheese wasn't always part of dinner, lending itself

more to less formal meals or casual snacking. It was sometimes served as part of the eighteenth-century *à la Française*
meal, sliding in between the second course with all its roast
meats, vegetables and plum puddings and sweet, ethereal
dessert. When the service style changed, becoming more
sequential, cheese sometimes stayed as a separate course, but
also started to morph into dessert. The Edwardian era was
that of the after-dinner savoury: intensely savoury, umami-
rich titbits which, like ice cream, cleansed the palate, but were
more manly and went better with port. Savouries were very
British, and more often than not based on cheese.

In the 1920s and 1930s, the British definition of dessert
broadened to include dishes which had previously been
served as part of the main march of the meal, such as sweet
puddings, fruit tarts, various forms of creamy confections
such as trifles and blancmanges, jellies and moulded cakes.
For some, the distinction was partially retained by calling all
of this 'the sweet course', shortened later to simply 'sweets',
leaving potential room for a ripe piece of fruit or an ice still
to come. For others, dessert came to be the catch-all term for
anything sweet.

Cheese now got stuck in a no-man's land. Before, after,
with or instead of? The British went one way, the French,
following a similar trajectory but lacking the savoury tradition, went another. Stilton and port became a mainstay for the
gentlemen's half hour on their own after dinner, the dishes
cleared, and the women having departed to drink tea in line
with lingering, if increasingly outmoded, social convention.

None of this was exclusive to Christmas, but below the level of the habitual port-and-Stilton-eaters it helped lend the habit an air of luxury. If Christmas was about pushing the boat out, expensive cheese was at least a good option, even if it wasn't a true priority.

There were other factors, however, in the association of cheese and Christmas, especially for the middle and working classes. Lipton's did much to promote the link, making the arrival of a series of gigantic cheeses into a regular December publicity stunt. Modern British towns might start Christmas with a vaguely heard-of ex-celebrity switching on the civic light display. Thomas Lipton gave his potential customers a circus elephant parading a massive block of Cheddar through the streets. The promotion of cheese as a Christmas food has continued ever since. Sadly, cheese parades are no longer part of it, and ever more outrageous flavours of Wensleydale (eggnog! Gingerbread! Champagne!) really aren't a match.

SUGGESTED BILL OF FARE FOR 25TH DECEMBER (1807)

John Simpson, *A Complete System of Cookery*[69]

FIRST COURSE.

Soup Santé
Removed with FISH, removed with *A Turkey, roasted.*

Semels and Poivrade Sauce.	Beef Collops à la Tortue, and Truffles.
Three Sweetbreads larded, glazed, and Asparagus Peas.	A Fowl à la Daube larded, and Mushrooms.
Three Chickens boiled, and Sauce à la Reine.	A Leg of Lamb and Tomata Sauce
Soup, removed with Fish, removed with a Bacon Chine, roasted	Soup, removed with Fish, removed with a Haunch of Venison.
A Neat's Tongue glazed, &c. and Greens.	Three Chickens and Celery Sauce.
Two Rabits à la Oporto larded, & Sorrel Sauce.	Grenadines and Endive.
A Souties of Mutton and Cucumber.	Petit Pâtés.

Frame.

Giblet Soup à la Tortue,
Removed with FISH, removed with
A Sirloin of Beef.

SECOND COURSE.

Four Partridges.

Caramell Basket with Pastry.	Chantilly Basket.
Brocoli with Brown Sauce.	Jerusalem Artichokes and White Sauce.
Cheese Cakes.	Mince Pies.
Spinach and Croutons.	French Beans.

Six Snipes.	Frame.	A Pheasant.

Asparagus.	Red Cabbage à la Allemand.
Mince Pies.	Apricot Tourte.
Ragout Mellé.	Mushrooms broiled.
Chantilly Cake.	Caramell Basket of Meringues.

Two Guinea Fowls, one larded.

NESSELRODE PUDDING

Jules Gouffé, 1867, *Le Livre de Cuisine* (translated by
Alphonse Gouffé, 1869, as *The Royal Cookery Book*)[70]

Described by one late-nineteenth-century author as a
'remarkable dish', Nesselrode pudding was something of a
quiet Victorian icon. Invented by a French chef called Mony,
adapted by Antonin Carême, copied by Eliza Acton and plagiarised by Isabella Beeton, it is a fabulous recipe. It is
incredibly rich, and utterly moreish. It was invented as a pas-
tiche on plum pudding, and for Christmas plum-pudding
deniers, or even those who just want a light(ish) end to a
hefty dinner, the flavours are properly festive-feeling. The
exact instructions of the original recipe show its origins as a
dish made in professional, high-end kitchens, although plenty
of simplified versions were around for those with fewer or
less-skilled servants.[71]

Original recipe:
Peel 40 chestnuts; blanch them in boiling water for five minutes;
peel off the second skin, and put them in a stewpan with 1 quart
of syrup at 16°, and 1 stick of vanilla. Simmer gently till the
chestnuts are done; drain, and press them through a fine hair
sieve. Put 8 yolks of egg in a stewpan, with ½lb of pounded
sugar, and 1 quart of boiled cream. Stir over the fire, without
boiling, till the egg begins to thicken; add the chestnut purée and
press the whole through a tammy cloth, into a basin, and add

1 gill of Maraschino. Stone ¼lb of raisins, and wash and pick ¼lb of currants; cook both together, in ½ gill of syrup at 30°, and 1 gill of water; drain, and let them cool. Put a freezing-pot in the ice; pour in the chestnut cream, and work it with the spatula; when it is partly frozen, add 3 gills of whipped cream, and continue working with the spatula until the cream is frozen; then add the currants and raisins, and put the pudding into an ice-mould; close it, and put some butter on the opening, to prevent any salt or water penetrating inside; imbed the mould in ice, and let it remain therein for two hours. Make the sauce as follows: put 3 gills of boiled cream in a stewpan, with 8 yolks of egg, and ¼lb of pounded sugar; stir over the fire, without boiling, till the egg begins to thicken; take off the fire, and stir for three minutes more; strain the custard through a tammy cloth, and add ½ gill of Maraschino. Put the sauce on the ice until it is very cold, without freezing. Turn the pudding out of the mould on to a napkin, on a dish; and serve with the sauce in a boat.

Serves 6–8
85g/3oz currants
85g/3oz raisins
90ml/3floz maraschino
1.2 litres/2 pints single cream
1 vanilla pod
225g/8oz caster sugar
1 tin of ready-cooked chestnuts (approx. 40 chestnuts)
4 egg yolks

Sauce (optional)
4 egg yolks
70g/2½oz caster sugar
300ml/10floz cream
3 tbsp maraschino

Put the currants, raisins and maraschino in a pan and bring to the boil. Simmer low for 5 minutes and leave to cool. Drain, keeping the maraschino. Infuse the cream with vanilla by simply putting the vanilla pod and cream with half of the sugar in a saucepan and bringing to an extremely gentle simmer. Remove from the heat and leave for 30 minutes.

Remove the pod and bring the cream back to a simmer. Purée the chestnuts by pushing them through a sieve or putting them in a food processor (you can use ready-prepared purée, but it is far too sweet, and mucks up the balance). Whisk the egg yolks and the rest of the sugar and pour over the cream, whisking. Put the mixture back on the heat and heat gently to thicken (do not let it boil). Add the chestnut purée and maraschino from the fruit.

Put the mixture into an ice cream maker (or you can use a bowl of ice and salt, as per the nineteenth century). Churn until it starts to set, then throw in the dried fruit. Churn until fully set. You can serve it now, or to be properly Victorian (and for ease of serving as part of a large and frantic meal), mould it. A pewter pineapple mould would be ideal, but you can use whatever you have to hand (a loaf tin, for example). Set it in the freezer for a few hours.

To make the sauce, simply make a custard with the egg yolks, sugar and cream, and add the maraschino off the heat.

Georgian Christmas: shrunken in the girth

The Georgian Christmas was a mixed bag. Beloved by the middle classes as a great tradition of ye olde Englande, yet simultaneously looked upon by some members of the aristocracy as a bit old-fashioned and (whispered) plebeian, there's a definite ambivalence in contemporary descriptions. Mentions of the word Christmas in print declined, and, more pertinently, so did the opportunity to celebrate it. In 1761 the Bank of England closed on forty-seven days of the year – by 1834 it was down to four. Shops which had fought to stay shut on Christmas Day in the 1640s now opened, at least on Christmas morning, so that people could buy provisions for their Christmas dinners.

For the very wealthy, the bon-ton who set fashion and owned stately homes, Christmas was a conundrum. It still had connotations of disorderliness and danger, and was rather rural and muddy. The idea of retreating to the country to feast all and sundry was a bit much. On the other hand, if you stayed in London, or headed to a fashionable resort, it was a great excuse for socialising and dinner-giving. Game was in season, and with winter fully set in it was a chance to showcase one's wealth through an ostentatious display of unseasonal fresh produce. Dinner was served *à la Française*, a highly intricate serving style in which a multitude of dishes were placed simultaneously on the table, in two main courses, with fruit, ices, nuts and other sweet things such as biscuits forming a final dessert course. Menus of the time include asparagus peas, French beans, asparagus, cucumbers, endives, apricots, raspberries and gooseberries, among others, and pineapple was also popular, forced in hotbeds fuelled by manure (the heat from the decaying manure helped ripen a decidedly exotic fruit which was, for a while, a real mark of wealth and the ability to employ skilled gardeners). The biggest dinners weren't always on Christmas Day itself, though, and, while the Twelve Days were now simply lines in a ballad, the festivities (or at least the eating) were spread over a lengthy season.

This didn't just apply to the aristocracy, either. Parson James Woodforde, living in Norfolk, recorded attending regular 'Christmas' dinners, but not always on Christmas Day. Visitors came, and visits were made in return. With fewer servants to cater them, his meals were smaller, usually centred around beef and plum pudding. Sometimes he hosted 'poor old people'.[72] Open-house hospitality was a thing of the past, but social obligations weren't. Jane Austen presented both sides of the debate in *Emma*. In the jolly corner was Mr Elton, 'At Christmas everyone invites their friends all about them, and people think little of even the worst weather. I was snowed up at a friend's house once for a week. Nothing could be pleasanter,' while Mr Knightley, possibly reflecting the view of the friend in question, complains of 'going in dismal weather, to return probably in worse, 4 horses and 4 servants taken out for nothing but to convey 5 idle shivering creatures into colder rooms and worse company than they might have had at home'. The latter was far from a minority view: others complained of the exhaustion and expense of endless entertaining, or of the increasing commercialism.

The custom of giving Christmas boxes, with money or useful gifts, to servants and tradespeople, was the cause of a lot of moaning. The term Boxing Day was first recorded toward the end of the period, as the 26th December was the customary day for the giving of boxes. But it was a system open to abuse. Householders complained of extortion, fearing that if the box wasn't deemed good enough, next year's sausages would be more meal than meat, and that the milkmaid would spit in the cream. It was all sufficiently dismal that even Charles Lamb, an enthusiast for Christmas, admitted that 'Old Christmas is a coming, to the confusion of Puritans, Muggletonians, Anabaptists, Quakers, and that Unwassailing Crew. He cometh not with his wonted gait, he is shrunk 9 inches in the girth, but is yet a Lusty fellow.'[73]

The already established foods of Christmas continued to be important. Mince pies, plum pudding, turkey and other fowl were eaten across the winter, though mince pies clustered more about Christmas itself than did the others. Beef was the dominant Christmas meat, though, served with the pudding, and in 1823 one visitor noted that '*This English custom of having a particular fare for this particular day is perhaps without exception the most universal of any that prevails in the country. Probably there is not a single table spread on Christmas day that is not furnished with roast beef and plum-pudding*'.[74] It wasn't unique to Christmas, but served, along with plum pudding, at any celebration which needed a bit of a patriotic yen. Beef was symbolic of Britishness, it was the meat which sustained armies and created, according to satirists, the doughty Britisher. John Bull was often portrayed as a butcher, and the British revelled in their meaty reputation abroad.

Putting on a good spread was important at every social level, along with music-making and other entertainment. 'The Humours of Christmas Holidays', one of a series of popular ballads in the 1790s, summed it up with:

Now the merry days of Christmas plays
Are coming to cheer our hearts,
See tables spread, from foot to head,
With plumb puddings, pies and tarts;
Nice hams and fowls, and punch in bowls,
In every beer house found,
Whilst fiddlers they sweet music play,
And jovial songs go round.

Not a great deal of this was family-friendly. Another Christmas ballad tells the cautionary tale of Letty, a maid who nips off with her lover after her feast of plum puddings, mince pies, pasties and a not inconsiderable amount of 'nappy cups of genrous juice':

Venus now hangs her Lamp on high / And gives the signal from the Sky / They view her Glories from afar / And follow the conducting star.

Not far remote a Churchyard lay / to this they bent their impious Way / And there (unheard of scene of lust!) / She lays her Honour in the Dust.

But Fame it seems in no ways approving / Th'Indecent Trade of Coffin Shoving / Or that he should impurely ground her / With such Memento Moris round her.

And vilely practice immorality / Amidst such emblems of Mortality / Spitefully told the merry Tale / To relish the next evening's Ale.

Christmas kiss and tell, 1730s style.

Slightly more suitable for children (albeit not by modern standards) was snapdragon, a game involving a platter of currants soaked in brandy and set on fire. Players had to grab as many as they could before the flames died. An alternative was flapdragon, which also involved flame, this time at the mouth of a tankard from which the intrepid reveller drank. More muted edible delights were on offer at Windsor in 1800, when Queen Charlotte imported the German custom of

Christmas trees. One contemporary report described how 'among other amusing objects for the gratification of the juvenile visitors, in the middle of the room stood an immense tub with a yew-tree placed in it, from the branches of which hung bunches of sweetmeats, almonds, and raisins, in papers, fruits, and toys, most tastefully arranged, and the whole illuminated by small wax candles. After the company had walked round and admired the tree, each child obtained a portion of the sweets which it bore, together with a toy, and then all returned home quite delighted.'[75]

When Queen Victoria ascended the throne, in 1837, trees of this type were still unknown beyond German immigrants and their families, of which she, of course, was one – as a child she'd grown up with Christmas trees. Christmas was taken for granted, a festival with church-going for some, and feasting for all (unless you were in the workhouse, in which case, tough luck). The accession of a vaguely pretty, and certainly innocent, eighteen-year-old girl was seen as the start of a new era after decades of lecherous old men. It would also prove to be key to Christmas, and to its dinners.

WHIPT SYLLABUB

'A Lady', 1836, *The Cook's Complete Guide*[76]

One of the mainstays of the dessert table, whipt syllabub was also a good party pick-me-up as well as being used on trifles. Seventeenth-century recipes had called for the cook to milk a cow into the alcohol, which could be cider, beer or wine, depending on the region and the recipe. However, it seems unlikely this was done with any frequency, merely plagiarised without thinking. By the late Georgian era, instructions were more practical, though, as here, did tend to assume familiarity with the technique. It's a dish we've completely lost now, replaced in the course of the nineteenth century by 'everlasting syllabub', which was more like the versions we know today.

Original recipe:
Take a quart of cream, a pint of white wine, the juice of a lemon, and one or two Seville or China oranges, with a large glass or two of brandy, a gill of orange flower water, and pounded sugar. Whip it up well, and as the froth rises take it off, and lay it on the back of a sieve to drain.

Serves 10–15, depending on the size of your glass and strength of your wrist
600ml / 1 pint single cream
300ml / ½ pint sweet white wine

The juice of 1 small lemon
The juice of 1 orange
25ml/1fl oz brandy
2 tbsp orange flower water
4 tbsp caster sugar

Pour everything into a very large bowl and mix with a spoon. Now raise the froth, for which a seventeenth-century chocolate whisk is ideal, but a modern balloon whisk will do. Don't whisk it. Hold the shaft of the whisk between your palms and roll it back and forth, fast. You should get bubbles forming on top of the cream. Once the whole surface is thick with froth (like bath foam), spoon it gently off and lay it on a sieve to dry out. A drum sieve works best. Do as much as you can cope with doing, then leave the sieve in a fridge for at least 15 minutes but up to a day to dry.

To serve, simply fill a glass a third full with the cream mixture and then heap the foam into the glass to form a steeple. It is very delicate, so be gentle. Eat with a spoon.

You can vary the alcohol, and it is particularly whizzy with red wine used for some glasses and white for others. Sherry, port and ginger wine all work well.

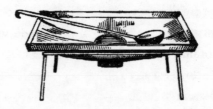

Sauces and other such stuff

Somebody, somewhere, in the eighteenth century, accused the British of having sixty religions and only one sauce.[77] The sauce in question was called melted butter sauce (often abbreviated simply to melted butter). It was not, however, just butter, melted, but was a mixture of butter, flour and water which formed a silky, shiny, sauce. Utterly ubiquitous at the time, it remained the standard British sauce well into the twentieth century but, in the changed landscape of post-war Britain, then completely disappeared.

It is a loss worth mourning, for it was simple to make, satisfyingly bland as a base and infinitely versatile in use. At the Christmas (and any other) table it could be boosted with lemon or vinegar for vegetables, anchovy or other ketchups for fish and meat, capers for mutton, and herbs or vegetables as desired. It was also used as a base for sweet dishes, with the addition of sugar and flavourings. Recipes abounded for savoury and sweet sauces made from scratch, but melted butter was tenacious, its appeal to the middle classes unassailable. That isn't to say it was always made well, however. Maria Rundell's comment on her recipe in 1808 was 'to melt butter, which is rarely well done, though a very essential article'. She would doubtless have been aghast at some 1930s recipes, which inevitably replaced butter with margarine (just don't), though she did agree with later writers that using milk as well as water was sometimes an improvement. In some ways, it was this which killed it off – for once a 1930s-style melted butter sauce is made entirely with milk, it is the same as a white sauce – which by then was also a bechamel sauce – in which the ghost of melted butter (sort of) survives today.

Britain did have other sauces, though admittedly most were derived from gravy. Gravy remains the most served sauce on the Christmas table, and, like melted butter, is both deceptively simple and subject to terrible abuses. At its most basic it is simply the pan juices from a roasted joint, deglazed with stock, defatted, seasoned and served. It is peculiarly British, mainly because no other country had quite such an obsession with roasting, and, like many of the dishes which became embedded in the national repertoire, was a mainstay of recipe books in the eighteenth and nineteenth centuries. 'Good Gravy' was as important as melted butter, but more expensive to make well, relying on obtaining good meat, and having access to the means by which to roast it. By the middle of the nineteenth century many recipe writers were advocating shortcuts, from thickeners to relying on separately made stocks. It was, according to the French, 'primitive', and part of the bourgeois repertoire. By the 1880s, the time-poor cook could simply buy a tin of meat essence and follow the instructions to make it into gravy (a few teaspoons of essence, some vaguely flavoured water, brown roux and maybe a spoon of mushroom catsup or sherry – but be warned, 'cooks too often spoil gravies by adding too much wine').[78] It is still a national obsession, and deservedly so for, done well, it is sublime.

The other major savoury sauce at Christmas, one which remains a minority choice, but a consistent one, is bread sauce. Breadcrumbs have been used to thicken sauces since at least the Roman era, lending bread sauce a true antiquity. However, early printed recipes for bread sauces to go with roasted birds (including game) vary considerably. One 1675 example involves claret, orange juice and lemon peel along with the onion, seasonings and breadcrumbs.[79] But blander recipes were around: Richard Bradley's 1730s version is simply an onion boiled with breadcrumbs and a little butter in water, the onion to be removed before serving.[80] He called it 'pap sauce', linking it explicitly to baby food, which even its admirers admit is not that far from the truth today. By the mid-eighteenth century, milk was usual instead of water, and it was standard enough that recipe writers were content merely to advise it should be used, with no need to give a recipe.

Moving away from savoury sauces, the other major condiment to appear on the British Christmas table is cranberry sauce. Ostensibly American, the modern adoption of it with turkey comes directly from its appearance on American

Thanksgiving tables. However, the combination of a sharp, fruity sauce with a rich meat again has older roots. Sharp sauces have been used to cut through fatty meats for centuries, and the European relations of the American cranberry – bilberries, whortleberries and so forth – have been used in this way since the medieval era. Other sauces, such as Cumberland, and redcurrant, as well as jellies including medlar and quince, have similar properties.

There are sweet sauces, too, from custard to brandy cream, the majority far from exclusive to Christmas. The only sweet sauce with a real claim to the season is brandy butter, which slowly emerged as an accompaniment to Christmas pudding over the course of the early twentieth century. Brandy butter is a relatively late addition to the table – unsurprisingly, given the presence of Christmas pudding as part of the main meal for most of its history. It's arguable as to whether it even is a sauce, given its unyielding, unsubtle mass. Recipes started to appear in the 1880s, but it wasn't common for some decades. It was related to buttercream, which was an American import, again not particularly mainstream until at least the mid-twentieth century. Far more popular for a long time was wine sauce, which could be made in a wide variety of ways. However, and neatly coming full circle, the most common, at least by the 1930s, was a milk-based melted butter sauce, enhanced quite simply with sugar and, if the diner was lucky, spice, lemon peel and even a splash of fortifying Christmas spirit.

A bit about game, and the epic Christmas pie

Past Christmases were undeniably meaty. Commentators did occasionally show slight signs of discomfort, such as this, from 1894: 'If any exception can be taken to Christ-tide in England, it is to the enormous amount of flesh, fowl, etc., consumed. To a sensitive mind, the butchers' shops, gorged with the flesh of fat beeves [beef], or the poulterers, with their hecatombs of turkeys, are repulsive, to say the least. It is the remains of a coarse barbarism, which shows but little signs of dying out.'[81] But in the main, meat remained the benchmark for a good Christmas, not least because for so many people it was scarce during the rest of the year.

For the wealthy, though, there was meat and there was meat. Game, preferably hunted and killed on one's own estate, was the pinnacle of a full-blown dinner. Despite increasingly draconian game laws in the seventeenth and eighteenth centuries which sought to limit poaching, it was widely traded and highly sought after by the urban middle classes. Much of the venison illegally traded in London was poached by commercial gangs operating in Windsor Great Park.[82] One *Lady's Magazine* contributor in 1780 railed against the unfairness of attempts to deprive 'worthy citizens' of their 'annual hare', prepared with a 'most excellent pudding in their bellies'.[83] Game was most obviously present as a roast, legs and head on, and, in the case of birds, carefully laid on a piece of bread to soak up the juices and stop it sliding about. In season at Christmas were hares, partridges, pheasant, snipes, wildfowl (duck and teal), grouse and woodcock. The latter were especially prized, for they could be roasted without being gutted first (they defecate on take-off). Cooked in front of the fire on a hanging spit, they would drop their innards on to a carefully placed piece of bread about halfway through cooking, making for two meals in one – guts on toast and roast game bird.

However, while roast game was part of the Christmas spread, it was not specific to the season. Put it in a Christmas pie, though, and it very much was. By the seventeenth century Christmas pie meant game pie, and not just any game pie, for Christmas pies were immense. Hannah Glasse included a recipe for one in her 1747 *The Art of Cookery Made Plain and Easy*. It starts 'first make a good standing crust, let the wall and bottom be very thick'. She filled it with a pigeon inside a partridge inside a fowl inside a goose inside a turkey, all seasoned with the usual eighteenth-century flavours of mace, nutmeg, cloves, pepper and salt. But that wasn't the end of it, for to this five-bird behemoth she added a jointed hare, woodcock, 'more game, and what sort of wild fowl you can get'. They were all well covered in 'at least four pounds of butter' and baked, with a thick lid on top, for at least four hours. The thick crust – edible but hefty – was necessary for 'these Pies are often sent to London in a Box as Presents; therefore the Walls must be well built'.[84]

Glasse was heavily plagiarised in the decades that followed, as, in turn, were several of the authors who had copied her recipes. Her recipe had been called 'Yorkshire Christmas pie', and the title was copied along with the recipe. Yorkshire was already known for its rather simpler goose pies, so it was an easy association to understand. It was also sometimes called Yorkshire Christmas pot. By the nineteenth century, the name was set, and the pie itself gaining status. Not all recipes involved boning the contents – as with many historic pies, the outer case was treated as much as a vessel to cook in as something to consume with pleasure (though consumed it was, by lower status members of the household, the poor or, ultimately, as pigswill). What was universal was a desire to really go large. Glasse's version was big – but they got bigger. One late-eighteenth-century example was described as containing '2 bushels of flour, 20lbs of butter, 4 geese, 2 turkeys, 2 rabbits, 4 wild ducks, 2 woodcocks, 6 snipes, and 4 partridges; 2 neats' [calf's] tongues, 2 curlews, 7 blackbirds, and 6 pigeons'. Unsurprisingly 'It is supposed a very great curiosity … It was near nine feet in circumference at bottom, weighed about twelve stone, and will take two men to present it at table. It was neatly fitted with a case, and four wheels to facilitate its use to every guest that inclines to partake of its contents at table.'[85]

Queen Victoria was one of many aficionados of the Christmas pie, which peaked during her reign and died out along with other excesses of the era after the First World War. In 1857 the *Illustrated Times* published an engraving of her Christmas sideboard, with resplendent footmen parading through a door carrying a boar's head and a pie of such dimensions that four men act as its bearers. It may have been a slight exaggeration: a photograph of her Christmas sideboard from 1888 shows a pie which is enormous, but not quite that enormous. Groaning sideboards were fast going out of fashion by the end of Victoria's reign, maintained mainly at Christmas, and focused on such pies. One French chef remarked that despite the general over-abundance of food around Christmas, the rich gloried in providing a sideboard of truly gigantesque proportions.

For the Yorkshire pie, then, size was everything, dwarfing reality by some way. Charles Dickens deserves the last word for taking it to its ultimate peak in 'The Holly-Tree': 'Once I passed a fortnight at an Inn in the North of England, where I was haunted by the ghost of a tremendous pie. It was a Yorkshire pie, like a fort – an abandoned fort with nothing in it; but the waiter had a fixed idea that it was a point of ceremony at every meal to put the pie on the table. After some days I tried to hint, in several delicate ways, that I considered the pie done with; as, for example, by emptying fag-ends of glasses of wine into it; putting cheese-plates and spoons into it, as into a basket; putting wine-bottles into it, as into a cooler; but always in vain, the pie being invariably cleaned out again and brought up as before. At last, beginning to be doubtful whether I was not the victim of a spectral illusion, and whether my health and spirits might not sink under the horrors of an imaginary pie, I cut a triangle out of it, fully as large as the musical instrument of that name in a powerful orchestra. Human provision could not have foreseen the result – but the waiter mended the pie. With some effectual species of cement, he adroitly fitted the triangle in again, and I paid my reckoning and fled.'[86]

Roast potatoes

Roasties are on the edge of Christmas fare. Ubiquitous all year round, they really aren't a festive food. However, they are the most common dish to appear on the festive table, so in the spirit of completeness, it seems only fair to include a brief nod.

Potatoes were introduced to the UK, along with so many other foods, as part of the Columbian exchange in the late sixteenth century. They were slow to catch on. Their peeling skin and knobbly exterior looked suspiciously leprotic, and given one of the prevailing medical doctrines of the time was that foods gave visual clues as to what they did to you, it seemed wise to avoid the risk. They were also thought to be poisonous, as related to deadly nightshade, and the earliest varieties to be grown were weedy and bitter. It was not an auspicious start.

In the eighteenth century, however, growers and governments alike became increasingly interested in potatoes. They had a long heritage in South and Central America, where they'd been a staple for thousands of years, and were now a possible solution to the looming problem of mass starvation as the European population increased. Antoine-Augustin Parmentier, a Frenchman who'd been brought round to the cause of the potato while in prison in Prussia, tends to get most of the publicity for promoting the potato. Once back in France, he studied them, championed them and eventually planted up fields with ostentatious guards around them, so that the still-wary poor would break in and steal the crop. However, he was by no means alone, and, once the potato started to take off, consumption quickly soared.

Potatoes were cheap, easy and versatile. Over-reliance on them could be a killer when crops failed, though, and the Great Famine of the 1840s remains one of the darkest phases of Anglo-Irish history. But they featured on the tables of rich and poor alike, albeit cooked in very different ways. As Christmas food, though, the roast potato rules supreme.

Until the advent of closed ranges and roasting ovens, roasting meant cooked in front of the fire. In the nineteenth century recipes called 'roast' potatoes are more akin to baked versions today, cooked on or under the fire grate without fat. But the modern concept existed as well, with the potatoes par-boiled and added to the drip pan under the meat on its spit. Yorkshire pudding, previously known as fire or batter pudding, was cooked in the same way, benefiting equally from the heady mixture of fat and flavour which dripped steadily from the slowly turning meat.

In the twentieth century open-fire cooking gave way to ovens and roasting became synonymous with baking. A roast potato should be a textural and taste delight, crisped in fat and seasoned with salt, but they are the subject of fierce debate. To peel or not to peel, to coat with spice or semolina, to salt before or after, the kind of fat – proof, again, if any were needed, that the simplest things can be the most difficult to get right.

Stuff to stuff with

Stuffing is a highly personal thing. There's the desired flavour: sage and onion, apple, apricot and chestnut, breadcrumbs or meat, spicy or sweet. Do you add the liver, or leave it out (did you even get the liver with your bird of choice?). Then the positioning: inside the cavity of your roasted bird where it steams and goes all soggy, or baked separately in a bowl, to be crisp on top but risk drying out inside? And do you scoop it, slice it, or even serve it in individual ramekins?

Many of us think of pork when we think of stuffing. The general theme of pork, sage and onion, pushed with grim determination into the body of the bird, rules supreme. But having enough meat to stuff anything into, let alone make stuffing of, was a rare thing for much of the population for much of the past. Even at Christmas, when meat was the aspiration, for most families stuffing was the thing used to eke out the rabbit, mutton or brisket, and recipes were basic, using oats, breadcrumbs and suet as the base, flavoured with cheap spice and herbs.

Stuffing as we would recognise it developed in the late medieval era, initially as a close cousin to pie fillings. Although the term nominally existed, it was not much used. One early Tudor dictionary included it in its definition of the sadly now defunct word 'fartile', continuing, 'stuffing, that wherewith any fowle is crammed or franked'. By the seventeenth century, the more generally used name was forcemeat, from the French 'farce', to stuff. Recipes were wildly varied, depending on what was being stuffed, and there were fish forcemeats, meat forcemeats and fruit forcemeats.

The mixtures involved weren't just for filling deboned joints or gutted birds. They were used as inserts, stuffed under skin or into pockets in meat, but also as accompaniments, made into balls and used on skewers stuck in the joint, or laid around the outside of the dish. They weren't even limited to fish and meat. John Nott included a recipe 'to farce eggs' in his 1726 *Cook's Dictionary*. By 1830, Dolby's similarly encyclopaedic *Dictionary of Cookery* listed fifteen forcemeat recipes (including two pies, small puff pastry patties and specific recipes to accompany turtle, hare and baked soles). He also gave a generic recipe, based on chopped veal, ham, fowl or bacon, plus breadcrumbs, herbs, spice and eggs, to which other flavourings could be added: oysters, anchovies, basil, cayenne, allspice and shallots being just a few of his suggestions.

Veal was the go-to for upper-class forcemeats, though,

especially for galantines, the ultimate in stuffed meats (not to be confused with the modern use of 'galentine' for a platonic Valentine's Day, which involves no stuffing at all). Alexis Soyer gave several recipes for turkey galantines. In them the cook is required to bone a turkey and pack it with a basic forcemeat of veal and spice, pepped up with foie gras, or pistachios and truffles, before wrapping it, poaching it, and, when cool, decorating with aspic and fancy designs made of ham and truffles. One version, '*à la Volière*', goes further. Halfway through the recipe, the unwary cook is told 'you have saved one of the legs of the turkey'. This is covered with more forcemeat, sculpted carefully to replicate the 'real head and neck', at which point 'stick the two claws of a convenient-sized lobster in the sides for wings, and with the tail of the lobster form the tail of the bird'. For a final flourish, waves of aspic and croutons are added. (There's even a picture. It looks like an angry seagull with broken wings.)

Inevitably, the turmoil of the twentieth century put an end to the heyday of forcemeat garnishes and extreme meat sculptures. By the mid-twentieth century pork was replacing veal in meat mixtures, along with a gradual name change to the simpler 'stuffing'. In 1938 Florence B. Jack's *Cookery for Every Household* listed seventeen such recipes, which included sage and onion, chestnut and apple. Those called forcemeat were notably old-fashioned, as well as more upmarket, and were still based on veal, or intended specifically for game (or fried as balls for garnishing).[87] Many of the recipes are now very plain, among them a nut stuffing with pine nuts, butter, onion, breadcrumbs, cream and egg; a chestnut stuffing with sausage meat and breadcrumbs, and an apple stuffing for pork or goose.

Twenty years later, indexes which still included the term forcemeat simply referred the reader to stuffings. Invariably, they included ideas specifically for the Christmas turkey, which by now were generally based on chestnuts. Constance Spry gave three recipes for meatless chestnut stuffing for turkey, plus two more based on chipolatas. Her 'excellent' stuffing also threw in the turkey liver, fresh plums, pears and a glass of white wine. In the 1970s, Fanny Cradock, always on trend, gave recipes for turkey stuffing (bacon and liver, and sausage meat), capon (chestnuts with sherry and cream), chicken (more sherry, almond, chicken liver and pistachios), goose (sage and onion, and apple with pork) and the evocatively named 'stuffing for hard times' based on red wonder beans flavoured with ox-liver, onion, bacon and suet.[88] Her hot tip was to use a piping bag to get the stuffing into the bird. Today it would be the stuff of a thousand memes, but it does work.

Victorians: reinventing, reinterpreting, renaming

As the Victorian age got under way in the 1830s there were many underlying ideas which remain familiar today. Notions of hospitality, of conviviality, and of eating too much and getting drunk were already established and became even further embedded. Certain foods – roast beef and plum pudding, mince pies, turkey and brawn – were, despite declarations to the contrary, not universally eaten, due mainly to cost and accessibility, but they were linked overtly and increasingly exclusively to the festive season by most of the population. There were stirrings, already, of the changes to come: a re-evaluation of what Christmas should mean, of who should be involved, and of how much more could be sold off the back of it. In culinary terms, this was the grand age of codification, and that included Christmas dinner.

In 1843 Charles Dickens' *A Christmas Carol* was published.

It was not the first cautionary Christmas tale, nor would it be the last, but it was wildly popular and remains one of the best-known seasonal stories. But Dickens did not cause Christmas to be reborn. Nor did Prince Albert, who, when he married Queen Victoria, brought with him not just a German sense of correctness, but also added to her love of Christmas trees. Both were part of a zeitgeist, a real feeling that Christmas should be focused on family, on the home and on charity. There was a strong and slightly saccharine strand of false nostalgia running through the whole thing, from Washington Irving's peacock pie in a heavily mythologised manor house, to William Sandys' 'Christmastide', with pictures contrasting old (drunk) and new (family) Christmases.

The Christmas of the mid-Georgian period was hastily rewritten as one of hospitality and goodwill, now apparently sadly lacking. The era before the Civil War was even more revered, seen as a rural idyll full of rosy-cheeked peasants in a time of rapid urbanisation and industrialisation. *Punch* asked its readers 'what have you done, this "merry Christmas", for the happiness of those about you, below you? Nothing? Do you dare, with those sirloin cheeks and that port-wine nose, to answer – nothing?'[89]

Food was everywhere. It was almost obligatory for the various literary outpourings which went into the revision of Christmas to dwell on eating, linking the foods of the season ever more closely to Christmas itself. In *A Christmas Carol*, the Ghost of Christmas Present is surrounded by plum puddings, sausages, punch bowls, mince pies, joints of beef, brawn, turkeys, geese, twelfth cakes and (foreground in the accompanying illustration) a highly festive dead hare. Meanwhile the *Illustrated London News* published articles – quickly paraphrased in the worldwide press – on Christmas at Windsor Castle, extolling the virtues of the Queen's beef, turkey, woodcock pie and generally groaning tables.

But even while certain foods became increasingly set in stone, in reality menus, at least for the rich, remained varied. Charles Francatelli's ideal menus in his 1842 *Modern Cook* were simply labelled as 'December' and, as was the norm for all upper-class meals, started with soup (one of which was always game) and fish before going on to dishes including veal, mutton, white puddings and pork. More seasonally, he also listed lots of game. Ham with Brussels sprouts crept in, as did roast turkey à la Chipolata (stuffed with chestnuts, accompanied with fried sausages, streaky bacon, more chestnuts, and a typically bewildering ragout made of more chestnuts, plus (among other things) cockscombs, truffles, mushrooms, as well as turned carrots and turnips all braised in a rich, meaty gravy enriched with Madeira). His second-course suggestions ranged from roast game to mince pies, plum pudding and vegetables, including Jerusalem artichokes, potatoes, endives and spinach.

The Victorian dinner slowly morphed from the old *à la Française* style with simultaneous serving of many dishes, to the newer, *à la Russe* sequential style akin to a modern-day tasting menu. By 1901 suggested Christmas (no longer December) menus for the upper classes were both longer and more uniform. Turkey or goose was a given, beef and game still important. Plum pudding, mince pies and potatoes were also invariably present, though they were still surrounded by many other options if the gathering was big enough. But meals of this type required work, and people. Upper-class kitchens were staffed by at least four people, and even the lower middle classes, able to afford only the bare minimum of two or three servants, employed a cook.

Lower down the social scale, in the working-class households which made up the majority of the population, the various dishes deemed fit for a Christmas dinner were more stripped back, served simultaneously as they always had been. A joint of meat, two dishes of vegetables, a pudding and a sauce were the basic elements. It made for a good spread, and it felt traditional, and realistically no one below the upper middle classes served more than two courses anyway. Unless a household could afford parlourmaids they were serving themselves, which made any idealised serving style involving ferrying multiple courses to and from the kitchen laughable. Many elements were bought in, easily elevating what was essentially a glorified Sunday roast to something more suitably celebratory.

The codification of Christmas dinner was well under way. Turkey was now associated very closely with Christmas and only Christmas. Recipes for roast turkey and ingenious ways to use up its endless leftovers started to dominate sections on the bird in newly published books, along with stuffings invariably based on chestnuts. With linear menus, the simultaneous serving of sweet dishes among the savoury meats died out. Plum pudding was rebranded Christmas pudding, moved to the end of the meal and its association with beef rapidly disappeared. Meanwhile rich fruit cake declined as a Twelfth Night party piece and became Christmas cake. Mince pies, too, became tied to Christmas and not just winter.

By the late Victorian era the ideal British Christmas meal was so established that it was hard to envisage anything else. The foods which appeared did so only once a year, and started to become heavily mythologised. Christmas foods were no longer the foods of the everyday, and were imbued with a sense of otherness, afforded a meaning far beyond their apparent worth. Ideals of tradition, stability and celebration collided with a delicious shiver of mild transgression, associations which would only grow when Victorian children grew up and looked back. Agatha Christie looked back on her wealthy pre-war childhood with a typical sense of nostalgia: 'The Christmas fare was of gargantuan proportions. I was a skinny child, appearing delicate, but actually of robust health and perpetually hungry! The boys and I used to vie with each other as to who could eat the most on Christmas Day. Oyster Soup and Turbot went down with undue zest, but then came Roast Turkey, Boiled Turkey and an enormous Sirloin of Beef. The boys and I had two helpings of all three! We then had Plum Pudding, Mince-Pies, Trifle and every kind of dessert. During the afternoon we ate chocolates solidly. We neither felt, nor were, sick! How lovely to be eleven years old and greedy!'[90]

The British Christmas dinner, as increasingly rigid as it was, was also spreading outwards. When Christmas cards first started to take off, in the 1870s, designs included robins drunk on punch with a cat creeping in to take advantage, monster Christmas puddings with terrifying faces, walking root vegetables, and humans dressed as rats roasting an actual rat over a fire (Victorian Christmas cards are great). They, and the continued popularity of British-published cookery books in the wider English-speaking world, all helped to spread the norms of the British Christmas dinner far beyond the confines of the UK itself. In countries such as Australia, India and New Zealand, hardly climates which lend themselves to huge, heavy roast dinners in December, determined British immigrants stuck doggedly to what they were used to, despite the potential for digestive difficulties: 'merry Christmas, with the roast beef in a violent perspiration, and the thermometer at 110° in the shade! ... it may be a rank heresy, but I deliberately affirm that Christmas in Australia is a gigantic mistake.'[91] 'Tradition' had a lot to answer for.

Despite the general fervour, there were dissenting voices. George Bernard Shaw, ever a cheery soul, fulminated regularly on the subject: 'We must be gluttonous because it is Christmas. We must be drunken because it is Christmas. We must be insincerely generous; we must buy things that nobody wants, and give them to people we don't like; we must go to absurd entertainments, that make even our little children satirical; we must writhe under venal officiousness from legions of freebooters, all because it is Christmas – that is, because the mass of the population, including the all-powerful middle-class tradesmen, depend on a week of licence and brigandage, waste and intemperance to clear off its outstanding liabilities at the end of the year.'[92] However, his was a voice in the wilderness. While the idea of a family gathered safely in around a laden table wasn't necessarily the reality for Victorian families (especially those of the working class), it was the aspiration. If shopkeepers benefited, good for them. Christmas windows and Christmas shopping were fun. December was still pretty dreary, despite the gas lighting, and who wouldn't want to ogle a wall of Christmas puddings in the window of the local grocer?

BILL OF FAMILY FARE,
SUNDAY DECEMBER 25TH (1864)

Annie Griffiths, *Cre-Fydd's Family Fare*[93]

Breakfast
Minced meat pâté, broiled pork, fried eggs, hot cake

Dinner
Hare soup
Roast beef, horseradish, boiled fowls, tongue,
stewed celery
Brussels sprouts, potatoes
Plum pudding, mince pies
Stilton cheese, pulled bread

Kitchen
Roast goose, apple-sauce, greens, potatoes,
plum pudding

WASSAIL

Cassell's Dictionary of Cookery, 1892[94]

Drinking too much and behaving like a hooligan is one of the most time-honoured rituals of Christmas, pre-dating the Christianisation of the winter festivities by several centuries. Hot spiced alcoholic drinks weren't unduly common in the centuries when wassail was a large part of celebrations, and even if they started hot, the temperatures in the large halls and open orchards with which wassail was associated would quickly have rendered the bowl tepid, at best. By the time printed recipes started to circulate, traditions had changed, and hot ales, mulled wines and such like were very popular. This late-nineteenth-century recipe probably bears little resemblance to the wassails drunk in Tudor great halls, but it is nevertheless delicious. It works both as an eyebrow-raising pre-dinner alternative to cocktails, or as an accompaniment (or alternative) to dessert. You can use sherry, Madeira or any other fortified wine in place of the white wine. Be warned – it is very rich.

Original recipe:
The wassail bowl used in ancient days to be served specially on Christmas Eve. It was brought into the banqueting hall with songs and carols, and crowned with garlands. To make it, grate half a nutmeg, and put it into a saucepan with one clove, a quarter of an ounce of grated ginger, half a small blade of mace, an inch

of stick cinnamon, and two or three coriander and cardamom seeds. Pour upon these ingredients a teacupful of cold water, and let them boil. Then add two bottles of white wine, not sweet, and three-quarters of a pound of refined sugar. Pour the mixture into a large saucepan, and set it on the fire. Break the yolks of six and the whites of three eggs into the wassail bowl. When the wine is warm, mix a tea-cupful of it in a bowl with the eggs; when it is a little warmer, add another teacupful, and repeat until five tea-cupfuls have been used. Let the wine boil, and pour it upon the eggs, stirring briskly all the time to froth it. Core, but do not pare, six apples; fill the cavity with sugar, roast them, and throw them into the bowl. Serve very hot.

Serves 6–10

6 medium-sized eating apples such as Coxes, russets or
    Braeburns
6 tbsp brown sugar
3 tsp butter
½ tsp ground nutmeg
1 clove
1 tbsp ground ginger
1 blade of mace (or a pinch of ground mace)
1 stick of cinnamon
8 cardamom pods, hit to split
½ tsp whole coriander seeds
2 bottles of white wine – hock or similar
340g/12oz granulated sugar
4 egg yolks and 2 egg whites

Start by roasting the apples: core them, but don't peel them. Stuff the centres with a tablespoon of sugar, rub them all over with butter, and bake them on a greased baking sheet at 200°C/390°F for around 30 minutes until cooked through and very tender.

While they are cooking, put the spices in a pan with 150ml/5floz of water and bring to the boil. Add the wine and sugar and bring to a simmer. In a large heatproof serving bowl, whisk the eggs until light and frothy. Add a ladleful of hot wine, whisking well, and then another. Then add the rest of the wine, whisking – you should get a reasonable froth. Remove your apples from the oven and add them carefully to the bowl. Keep the wassail hot, and serve in mugs or teacups, breaking up the apples as you fancy.

Beyond the brassica

It is a tired trope to suggest that people didn't eat vegetables in the past. Of course they did (most people ate little but). But cookery books don't contain many recipes for them, and they don't usually appear on menus or table plans. This was partly because they were included in other dishes, and partly because it was taken for granted that people knew how to cook them (boiled, mainly, to be served with melted butter sauce) and that they would be present on the table. It is also because until the middle of the nineteenth century cookery books were aimed at the middle classes and above, and the food of the poor was unrepresented.

In the nineteenth century this changed. Books aimed at the working classes appeared, complete with vegetable cookery – but it was unrelentingly tedious and bland. In upper-class cookery, however, recipes for more interesting – or at least more fiddly – vegetable dishes appeared in books with more frequency, in the form of chapters on garnishes.

Dish presentation was changing in line with fashion and technology, particularly in terms of moulded foods. Garnish did not mean a token lettuce leaf or a tired sprig of parsley, but a full-on preparation of vegetables displayed with panache. Thus, red cabbage might be stewed with butter, white and black pepper, salt and vinegar before being pressed into a pyramid upon which to display meat cutlets. Chestnuts were stewed in consommé until the sauce thickened to a glaze, and used to form a border round a turkey. Time was money, and plain vegetables were hardly impressive except when out of season (asparagus remained a popular choice). However, with determined application of cutters and knives, and the addition of sauces to stick things together, even a turnip could be made to (literally) shine.

However, while they were omnipresent upon the table, at every social level, vegetables weren't prestigious, and weren't associated with celebratory feasts, including those at Christmas, in the way other dishes were. For the majority of the population, the vegetables on the Christmas table would have been those which were cheap and plentiful, prepared simply. Onions were a prime example, most often to be found in stuffings, but also eaten by themselves. The upper classes avoided them except in small doses, due to their anti-social effect on the breath. One Edwardian writer made this explicit: 'There are some who delight in the flavour of onions. I do myself – but then I am a bachelor. Politeness and onions form one of life's most persistent inconsistencies.'[95]

Many root vegetables were also in season, though some,

such as parsnips, were so associated with the poor and/or feeding horses that eating them reeked of desperation. Nor could they be called Christmas foods, since they were eaten whenever obtainable, and then avoided if the eater became wealthy enough to have a choice. They remain surprisingly divisive, despite a modern resurgence.

One root which did have a claim to be Christmassy was the Jerusalem artichoke. Introduced from the Americas around the start of the seventeenth century, Jerusalem artichokes have nothing to do with Jerusalem – the name is probably a corruption of the Italian for sunflower, *girasole*, which the plants resemble. Never particularly mainstream, they were eclipsed by the standard potato in the eighteenth century and were largely confined to middle- and upper-class tables. They were roasted, fried, mashed and gratinated, but it was as a soup called Palestine soup that they appear most frequently on Victorian December menus. Given their infamous effect on the digestive system, it seems an unwise choice for those in tight corsets, but presumably the taste outweighed the risk. Perhaps their inclusion simply proves that flatulence has been part of the British Christmas for longer than we might think.

Brassicas were also in season: cabbage, broccoli and the various types of kale. Sea kale was the choice of the rich, as it required forcing and therefore showed a bit more effort and money. However, it was in the form of sprouts that brassicas really made their mark, and sprouts continue to be the one vegetable (other than potatoes) truly associated with Christmas today. Lauded for being 'tender, delicate-flavoured, and very nutritious', they are at their best in winter. However, even as they gained in popularity in the mid-nineteenth century one author admitted that 'their greatest drawback is that ... they are somewhat difficult to digest'.[96] They are particularly problematic when overcooked, which given the length of time some authors gave for vegetable cookery in the past, even allowing for different cultivars, does suggest bad times were in store for many a Victorian diner. Many books also suggested adding bicarbonate of soda to the cooking water, which keeps the green colour, but also destroys much of the nutritional value.

When sprouts first made their appearance is debatable. There are possible references from late-sixteenth-century Italy, but the recipes may just be calling for small cabbages. However, they were almost certainly first bred in Italy, and were grown in the UK by the late eighteenth century. The first printed recipes appeared in the 1840s. The ever-reliable Eliza Acton gave one for Brussels sprouts dressed 'in the Belgian way', boiled in salted water for 8–10 minutes, drained, and served on buttered toast with melted butter sauce. Charles Francatelli, who put them on several of his December menus in his 1846 *Modern Cook*, included recipes for them as a garnish (boiled, with white sauce flavoured with nutmeg and lemon juice), as a side dish (boiled, with velouté sauce and a decorative pastry border), and as part of a serving suggestion for a boiled tongue. Both he and Isabella Beeton also used them on their December menus as an accompaniment for a boiled ham.

Even in the twentieth century sprout recipes were no more

imaginative than most other vegetable cookery. Countess Morphy's suggestions in her 1936 *Vegetable Dishes* mainly centred around boiling and adding one or more of butter, cream, chestnuts and breadcrumbs. If none of that appealed, she also included an upgrade where they were boiled, puréed with butter, and mixed with milk-soaked breadcrumbs and egg yolks before being steamed in a well-buttered mould and served with cream sauce or gravy. At least there were glimmerings of a backlash against bad sprouts. Another 1930s chef lambasted the British habit of choosing supersized sprouts, adding 'more than any other form of leaf vegetable, sprouts suffer from the prevalent fault of those cooks who soak them in water and render them sloppy and unappetizing. With sprouts, as with other forms of the cabbage, more butter should be used and thorough draining is an absolute necessity.'[97] His recipes included the usual suspects of buttery sauces, chestnuts, sprout purée and white sauce as well as sprouts with bacon, sprouts with sour sauce (essentially lemon and cayenne), and chilled boiled sprouts.

Despite the love/hate relationship we seem to have with them, sprouts are a mainstay of the British Christmas dinner. Indeed, the last few decades have seen a sudden rush of love for them, as they are rescued from overboiling and revalued. Work blending modern high-yielding varieties with older, better-tasting types has also resulted in genuinely nicer vegetables. Finally, and in the face of years of abuse, we recognise that, done well, they really are the sweet and tender vegetable past cookery writers told us they could be all along.

QUEEN VICTORIA'S CHRISTMAS DINNER (1855)[98]

Potages

À la jardinière, crème au riz

Poissons

Turbot, filets de sole frits

Relevés

Les dindes rôtis farcies chipolatas

Entrées

Filets de carpe à la régence, côtelettes d'agneau chicorée,
suprêmes de volailles pointes d'asperges, paté chaude de
foie gras, escalopes de grouse, côtelettes de venaison

Contre flanc

Les filets de chevreuil rôtis, jambons glacé, choux de
Bruxelles, poulets à l'estragon

Rôts

Faisans, poulets

Entremets

Épinards au velouté, salmis de pluviers, vol au vent
d'abricots, macédoines de fruits, jambons au surprise,
flamaris d'orange

Relèves

Mince pies, souffles à la palfy

Buffet

Roast beef, roast mutton, baron of beef [this weighed
382½lb], brawn, boar's head, game pie, woodcock pie,
raised pie

[Dessert, as ever, was implicit.]

All aboard the turkey train

Around 70% of us sit down to roast turkey on Christmas Day, making it the most popular meat by far. But while its association with the season goes back almost as far as its introduction to the UK, its dominance of our festive tables is rather more recent.

Turkeys are native to Central America. In the wild they are renowned for being both aggressive and crafty, and were domesticated relatively late, between 1,500 and 2,000 years ago. Once brought into the farming system, though, they rapidly spread far beyond their original pecking grounds, and by the time Columbus and his fellow explorers arrived, they were also being enjoyed in North America and the Caribbean. Unlike many new world foods, their value was immediately recognised, and old world enthusiasm quickly kindled. By 1511 every ship leaving the Americas for Spain was ordered to bring back five breeding pairs, to kick start the turkey industry there. As usual for new world ingredients, they then spread throughout Europe. In France, Margaret of Navarre was raising them by 1534, and in England in 1541 they were named, along with cranes and swans, in sumptuary laws restricting their service to only one per feast.

William Strickland, a Yorkshire landowner and a captain on Sebastien Cabot's exploratory voyages to the Americas, is often credited for the introduction of turkey to England in the 1520s. He certainly enjoyed an association with them, successfully petitioning the crown to have a turkey added to his coat of arms in 1550, by which time most of his contemporaries would have recognised what it was. However, this was probably as much for their native characteristics and as a nod to his seafaring past as for his specific role in bringing them to the country. While many were directly imported from America, they were more often traded to Europe in a roundabout route via Turkey, hence their name in English. While other new world foods came with westernised versions of usually Aztec names (avocado comes from a word which was also used as slang for testicle), in this case no one in the old world appears to have considered simply adopting one of the names already in use by either Native Americans or the Aztecs.

Once established, turkey boomed. Their flesh was sweeter and more tender than other, equivalent birds, such as heron, swan, bustard and peacock, all of which were flamboyant things to put on a celebratory table, but whose taste was more challenging. They fitted into the category of big birds, which could feed many people, and whose plumage could be used as part of their presentation on the table. Their other-worldly looks were part of the charm. Wrinkled and dangly red facial protuberances (more correctly snoods and wattles), blue heads and (for the males) impressive beards sticking out of their breasts looked particularly excellent rearing out of a pie. Some early recipes included stuffing – oysters and truffles were popular – confiting in butter, and roasting, often with an onion sauce. They were also poached and, by the seventeenth century, soused (pickled). A whole, boned, pickled turkey was a pretty impressive thing, the perfect gift for that annoying friend who seems to have everything else.

Turkeys were not just for Christmas, but, given that as with all poultry they were at their best from September to March, they inevitably became associated with the biggest excuse for an almighty feast in that period. In 1573 Thomas Tusser called them 'Christmas husbandlie fare'. Ninety years later Robert May recommended a month's worth of feeding them up before eating: 'sodden barley is excellent, or sodden oats for the first fortnight, and then for another fortnight cram then in all sorts as you cram your capon and they will be beyond measure'. Carcasses would then be dry hung for at least a week. Domestication didn't suit everyone, though. French author and bon viveur Brillat-Savarin, who had tasted wild turkey after an exhilarating hunt in 1791, wrote that it was much better eating than its farmed counterparts, and suggested turkeys should be 'driven into woods and fields, to enhance the flavour, and bring it as nearly as possible back to the original species'.

It didn't happen. Instead, in the eighteenth century, turkey farming intensified. Norfolk provided most of those intended for London, with the roads into the capital rendered impassable in the run up to Christmas by the scraping of flocks of clawed feet, en route to the capital. Wings were clipped to stop them flying, and they scavenged for fodder on the stubble to either side. In 1724 Daniel Defoe toured East Anglia, writing of the turkey drives with amazement. At one bridge over the River Stour he did a back-of-an-envelope calculation, based on the numbers he was told crossed the bridge throughout the autumn. He concluded '150,000 in all; and yet this is one of the least passages'. Turkey was getting cheaper, demand was going up. One solution to the road issue was to fit leather shoes to the birds (or to make them walk through tar to coat their feet). But shoeing several hundred thousand aggressive turkeys was a challenge. Defoe also noted attempts to transport poultry more practically, on multi-storied wagons travelling day and night.[99]

By the nineteenth century turkey was terribly middle-class. In 1861 Isabella Beeton, never one to resist a grandiose flourish, declared that 'a Christmas dinner, with the middle classes of this Empire, would scarcely be a Christmas dinner without its turkey, and we can hardly imagine an object of greater envy than is presented by a respected portly pater familias carving, at the season devoted to good cheer and genial charity, his own fat turkey and carving it well'. The barbed ending was a warning to those pretenders who had not been brought up knowing how to carve, though, given her audience was largely newly middle-class housewives des-perately seeking instruction, she did give full instructions, just in case. By now coach transport was the norm. One com-mentator described how 'many a time have we seen a Norfolk coach with its hampers piled on the roof and swung from beneath the body, and its birds depending, by every possible contrivance, from every part from which a bird could be made to hang. Nay, we believe it is not unusual with the pro-prietors, at this season, to refuse inside passengers of the human species in favour of these oriental gentry who "pay better".'[100]

Further up the social scale, the affordability of turkey ensured it only played a secondary role on the table. Big game remained the pinnacle of desire. Right at the top of society, Queen Victoria's menus occasionally still included peahen on special occasions. Swan was particularly popular, and was still eaten as a feast bird for those who had their own flocks into the twentieth century. Old birds were tough, and those intended for the table were that year's hatchlings, fat-tened on grain and eaten just as their feathers started to become fully white.[101] As late as 1931 *The Times* carried adverts for 'Cygnets (young swans) supplied dressed for dinners and banquets, or alive for ornamental waters', in this case from the master of the Great Hospital in Norwich, long the centre of the swan industry.[102] But game in general was prized, still denoting status, as hunting remained tightly reg-ulated to favour landowners.

Even for the middle classes, game still beat turkey when it

was obtainable. Despite Beeton's warm words, her menu for December included turkey boiled with celery, a classic Victorian way of cooking it, putting the true focus on roast game birds. Roasting was the prestige method of cooking, being inefficient, fiddly, and requiring special equipment. Although it was theoretically possible to roast in an oven, its results were highly debatable, and most understood a roast to mean cooked in front of an open fire. This could be done with a spit-jack or smoke-jack driven by a fan up the chimney, turned by the draw of the fire, with a weight or clockwork-driven jack, or, in extremis (and not suitable for turkey), with a simple piece of rope or string. Preparing meat for roasting meant plucking or skinning not only the body or whole small birds and animals, but also the head and legs, and trussing them in highly specific ways. Hare, for example, had to be served with the ears on (perkily arrayed on top of the head), while rabbits lost their ears. Larger joints still needed careful attention, with brown paper or a paste of flour and water applied carefully to ensure even cooking.

Goose was particularly widely eaten at Christmas, especially by the working classes, being, like turkey, very seasonal. Goose clubs abounded, whereby the poor could pay into a fund all year, to receive a goose come Christmas. But roasting them posed problems: ovens were small or non-existent in working-class homes. Victorian literature is peppered with tales of queues outside bakers on Christmas morning, as people paid a small fee to put their dish of meat into the vast ovens of the bakery. It was still part of some people's

Christmases in the 1960s, and one baker from Barnsley remembered the men gathered around the oven waiting for their roasts to be ready, while they drank beer and avoided their wives preparing the rest of the meal back home.[103]

In post-war Britain, Christmas menus were much reduced, even for the rich. Shortage of staff to cook a range of meats, shortage of money after death duties, depression and war, and simple shortage of food all combined to focus attention on a few key dishes. One roast alone now sufficed, and, as domestic ovens got bigger, and domesticated turkeys smaller and cheaper, they took over from beef and chicken, goose and game. Images of glorious golden Thanksgiving turkeys from America, a land of glamour and no rationing, also cast a certain spell. Slowly, over the next few decades, turkey become the real, and not just the aspirational, choice for the majority. Their size remained more than the (now smaller) average family could consume at one sitting, but, as eating habits changed, and fridges changed the way in which the remains of meals could be stored, turkey leftovers became an intrinsic part of Christmas too. In other countries, turkey is still a quotidian autumnal meat, whereas in Britain it is rare outside Christmas. It could be suggested that, despite its popularity on December 25th, if we really liked it, we might eat it more than once a year.

Yule logs and other cakes

I f not rich fruit, what then for cake at Christmas? The choices, once varied, have narrowed over the last 150 years. In the twenty-first century, the main contender for a place on the festive table is a yule log, a comparative newcomer as an edible delight. The original yule log was an actual log. Its origins predate Christianity, and it was one of several pan-European customs, though it's unclear when some of the traditions surrounding it emerged. It was popularly supposed to be brought in and lit on Christmas Eve, using a saved piece of the previous year's log. Some Yorkshire families maintained the custom right up to the eve of the First World War, though the name was, by then, also applied to the edible version.

Cake yule logs are a nineteenth-century invention, with recipes appearing in both French and English books by the early twentieth century. Generally made from plain Genoise sponge rolled round a filling of jam or buttercream, and decorated with piped buttercream, they were supposed to resemble a fallen log. They could be plain, but for commercial confectioners they usually weren't. Pierre Lacam instructed cooks in 1902 to use pistachio nuts for moss, grilled almonds for dead leaves, and extra sponge bits made to look like artistic knots and twigs. Meanwhile Frederick Vine's fairly muted directions, written in 1907, were illustrated in the 1930s by photographs of exhibition logs designed to resemble specific species of tree (the birch one was particularly delightful).[104]

Plain by nature, but visually impressive, yule logs crept into books aimed at home bakers, where the details and basic presentation were essentially the same as for the professionals. Instead of piping the log with individual lines of buttercream, though, cooks were advised simply to 'mark it with the prongs of a fork to resemble a tree trunk'. Still, chopped pistachios were employed to represent moss and the ends piped to looked like tree rings. How far the aspiring hostess wanted to go was really up to her. The 1970s Cordon Bleu cookery course suggested both nineteenth-century style meringue mushrooms with more contemporary sounding instant-coffee-flavoured boiled marzipan (to make knots).[105]

Logs were only a starting point for filling a gap on the Christmas dessert table, albeit a popular one. Cookery book writers helpfully gave variations. The French favoured pâtisserie, from Lacam's upright version of the yule log made from stacked sponge roundels covered in praline buttercream, to *Larousse Gastronomique*'s yule clog, made of nougat and garnished with petits fours (the clog was also an alternative name for the original burning log). The British, meanwhile, preferred good, solid, cake.

In late Victorian Britain, yule was a term more widely applied to Christmas confections, many of which were highly regionalised – and dying out. There were large cakes, intended, like Christmas cake, for eating over the whole period of Christmas, rather than just as a course on one day. In Durham, Whitby and other northern areas, a large fruit cake was popular, lighter than the rich mixture used for Christmas (Twelfth) cake, and known as a yule cake. Confectioners advertised various forms, some designed to be broken up into individual portions, some with basic decoration, such as scoring across the top.[106]

There were smaller cakes, too, eaten as part of a tea or as a simple sweet course by the poorer classes. Yule dough (or doo or dow) was 'a cake made in the shape of a flattened baby, with currants, cloves, or peppercorns for the eyes, which bakers used formerly to manufacture, and present to their customers as little remembrances of the year'.[107] Variously described as pastry or bread dough with dried fruit and spice in, it fell into the category of other such cakes, like Eccles, lardy or scrap, made cheaply and rarely described in recipe books. One late-nineteenth-century collector of dying regional customs listed other variations on the theme, including yule-babies in Alnwick, finger-cakes in Glamorgan, and in Cornwall 'currant cakes … coloured with a decoction of saffron' made a bauble-like top called 'the Christmas'.[108] Pop ladies were a St Albans variant.[109]

There was also a range of similarly simple seasonal treats based on mincemeat, which found its way into everything. Many of these were sold at New Year, rather than being specific to Christmas Day. Pig hogs (Colchester, Leicestershire, Cornwall) were rather devilish little pasties, horned and tailed, which may originally have contained pork (or porcine mincemeat). Three-cornered godcakes were Coventry's take on them – and the list goes on.[110]

SUGGESTED CHRISTMAS DINNER MENU (1904)

Charles Herman Senn, *The New Century Cookbook*[111]

Palestine soup

Boiled turbot with green mousseline sauce

Mutton cutlets with spinach

Partridge hodge-podge

Roast sirloin of beef

Cauliflowers and potato croquettes

Roast turkey stuffed with chestnuts

Salad

Plum pudding

Port wine jelly

Mince pies

Cheese fritters

CHRISTMAS OMELETTE

Alfred Suzanne, 1904, *La Cuisine et Pâtisserie Anglaise et Américaine*[112]

The words 'mincemeat omelette' tend to conjure up a vision of Fanny Cradock in an evening gown, and she did, indeed, attempt to popularise it in the 1970s. But Cradock drew a great deal on the past, and her mincemeat omelette is merely a muted version of this, published seventy years before. (Remarkably, she doesn't flambé it, possibly for safety's sake on set and wearing artificial fibres.) Alfred Suzanne's rather sarcastic cookery book was written to instruct classically trained French chefs about the strange things the English and Americans did with their food. He commented that the English were fanatical about mincemeat, consuming vast quantities, mainly as pies, on the week of Christmas. He grudgingly admitted that mincemeat was surprisingly excellent, to the extent that the French might be missing out by not adapting it for use in their own, more elevated, offerings.

Original recipe:
After breaking the eggs into a bowl, beat them with two spoons of cream and the same of rum and cognac, a pinch of sugar and a very small pinch of salt. Proceed as with an ordinary omelette; but before rolling it up on itself, cover it with three spoons of mincemeat. When it is turned out onto a plate, pour over some

*rum and cognac, sprinkle with some fine sugar, and set it on fire
at the point of sending it to table.*

Serves 2, as a dessert or a punchy breakfast
5 eggs
2 tbsp cream (single or whipping)
2 tbsp rum or cognac
1 tsp caster sugar
Pinch of salt
55g/2oz butter
3–4 tbsp mincemeat, heated to cook the suet
To serve
3 tbsp rum or cognac
Caster sugar, to taste

Whisk the eggs with the cream, rum or cognac, sugar and
salt. Melt the butter in a thick-bottomed pan until foamy and
lower the heat. Pour in the eggs, and stir with a fork until
curds form (as if making scrambled eggs). Once the pan is
around half curds, stop stirring and allow the bottom to fully
set, leaving the top slightly runny. Gently add the mincemeat,
and flip one half of the omelette over the other, before sliding
the whole out on to a heated plate. Heat the rum or cognac
for the flambéeing. Immediately before serving, sprinkle
caster sugar over the omelette, top with the heated spirit and
set it on fire.

Rationing Christmas:
it's the thought that counts

By the 1930s, the British Christmas had settled into a recognisably modern pattern. While domestic service remained a huge employer, only around 5% of households maintained a full-time live-in staff, meaning that the majority of people could be in their own homes for Christmas (or at least part of it). The extensive train network meant travelling to spend Christmas with family was relatively easy, and the family-focused cosy Christmas so heavily promoted by the Victorians was now accepted as the norm. However, there were exceptions. In Scotland Hogmanay remained a more important occasion, and many Scottish households resolutely held out against a festival which still had a whiff of popery – and English hegemony – about it.

However, shops, media and the population themselves were enthusiastic participants in a season devoted to shopping, drinking and eating. Christmas foods now meant foods served only at Christmas and ignored for the rest of the year. But the exact menu remained flexible. McDougalls' 1935 'Christmas Cheer' contained recipes for Christmas cake decorated with marzipan and royal icing, mincemeat (and mince pies), treacle toffee, trifle, brandy snaps, roast turkey and duck, boiled tongue and ham and sausage rolls. Meanwhile, Elizabeth Craig's 1937 Christmas menus all included Christmas pudding with a boozy sauce as well as roast potatoes – but the other elements varied considerably, with roasts ranging from beef to goose, and vegetables from spinach to celery and stewed red cabbage. Just three years later all of this would be swept aside, as not only food but fuel came under government control, and the heady days of hours of roasting and unlimited raisins became a distant memory.

Christmas 1939 was quite jolly, war and blackout restrictions aside. Rationing was promised, but not yet in place, and although supplies of imported fruit such as oranges and pineapples had dried up, most things were freely available. However, between the Blitz and the rationing of key ingredients including fat, sugar and meat, by 1940 dinner had already suffered drastic change. The Ministry of Food increased the sugar and tea ration the week before Christmas (but cut that of meat), meaning that puddings and cakes were still theoretically possible. The Stork wartime cookery book's rather optimistic wartime Christmas cake included nearly a kilo of dried fruit (unrationed but scarce), and two-thirds of one person's sugar ration for the week, along with 4 eggs. More practically, several magazines carried suggestions for festive sandwiches, to be eaten in an air raid shelter. Given that fires were still burning across Manchester after a series of raids early in the morning of Christmas Eve, a double-layer sandwich of tinned meat and Marmite was possibly the more practical option.

In 1941 the points system came in, allowing an illusion of choice, and mainly made up of tinned or dried foods imported under the lease-lend agreement with America. By now eggs were also on the ration, and recipe writers hastened to come up with reasonable solutions for eggless fruit cakes. Many are genuinely good, though they tend to rely on other ingredients such as cocoa powder and milk (also rationed), along with increasingly scarce sweet spices. Others were less palatable – custard powder does not work in place of eggs, and although there were rumours that paraffin could be used in place of other cooking fats, those who tried it tended to disagree. Then there was flour. It remained unrationed, but was now exclusively 'national flour', which was wholemeal, and fortified with calcium and other vitamins.

Dried egg powder (one packet, equivalent to twelve eggs, every two months) was touted as a saviour and was best used in cakes, since its flavour is best described as a heady mixture of wet cardboard and sulphur. Enterprising cooks could also attempt mock marzipan (made with haricot beans, rice or soy flour and relying on virtually unobtainable almond essence), and mock cream (margarine, sugar and milk, all rationed). Inedible accessories were vital to achieve anything like a festive result, but nevertheless people made a huge effort, especially if they had children to impress: 'our Christmas cake was made from American dried eggs and fruit and covered with soya flour, serving as a mock almond paste and white icing made with guess what, dried milk powder. It tasted absolutely revolting but looked nice. I remember one particular gem made by my innovative mother in the form of a house. It was square and set on a large green painted board. All around it in the garden were little Eskimos sliding on a pond-like mirror, trees and Father Christmases. I don't know how she did it. It was a true work of art.'[113] The Ministry of Food released extra suet for Christmas in 1941, meaning that pudding could be on the menu, but since dried fruit was now restricted too, the results were more carrot than anything else. Carrots were a recurring theme. The Ministry of Food admitted that for dessert there would be 'no gay bowls of fruit', but, as resolutely upbeat as ever, declared that 'vegetables have such jolly colours. The cheerful glow of carrots, the rich crimson of beetroot, the emerald of parsley – it looks as delightful as it tastes'.[114]

Meat remained a perennial problem, but with more people keeping chickens and rabbits, by 1942 both elderly fowl and young coneys appeared on menus. Those with large estates, of course, suffered far less, with seemingly endless supplies of game, including venison. Recipes abound for mock goose and duck (sausage meat bulked out with the inevitable potato), but a small, vaguely meaty shape wasn't exactly a centrepiece. Vere Hodgson, a charity worker in London, commented glumly that 'we are pretty well on our beam ends as far as Christmas fare is concerned. No chance of turkey, chicken or goose – not even the despised rabbit. If we can get a little mutton that is the best we can hope for.'[115]

Vere wasn't the only person who came to regard mutton as a Christmas treat. With the end of the war in 1945 the lease-lend agreement with the States also ended, and even the hated dried egg supply got shaky. A succession of poor harvests led to both bread and potatoes going on the ration for the first time in 1946. Food supplies only started to recover in 1948, by which time almost everything except meat was heading back to pre-war levels. The meat situation was made worse by rising prices, which meant that the ration, which was set on price rather than weight, was even more diminished. Even Winston Churchill ate roast mutton for lunch on Christmas Day 1949 (though he managed cold turkey, ham, Christmas pudding and mince pies for dinner – the turkey was a gift from America). But things were looking up. Gradually rationing ended: dried fruit in 1950, sugar and sweets in 1953, and finally butter and meat in 1954.

Rationing Christmas dinners were sparse and makeshift. But the era was a defining one. So much focus was put on making some form of merry despite the bombs, the anxiety and the shortages that when it all ended, the festival, along with the foods which had been so unobtainable for so long, was embedded even more deeply into the national psyche. Even today the idea of a Blitz Christmas conjures up paper chains and tinned turkey in a tube station. But paper was also rationed – and when cans of turkey were available, they used a whole month's points.

TWO FAMILY CHRISTMAS DINNERS (1937)[116]

Tomato soup
Roast sirloin of beef, Yorkshire pudding, roast potatoes,
buttered green peas
Plum pudding, brandy custard sauce
Dessert

*Note – serve peas with grated horseradish. Add a chopped
carrot to the peas. Serve celery all through the meal.*

*

Onion soup
Roast stuffed chicken, bread sauce, roast potatoes,
buttered spinach
Christmas pudding, rum butter
Dessert

*Note – garnish chicken with grilled rolls of bacon, or baked
chipolata sausages. Serve potato crisps instead of roast
potatoes if liked.*

WARTIME CHRISTMAS CAKE

Elizabeth Craig, 1941, *Cooking in Wartime*[117]

Wartime recipes were a mixture of sensible suggestions based on poverty cookery from the past, and more far-fetched solutions dreamt up in desperation and longing for pre-war largesse. With sugar, fat, dried fruit and fuel rationed, and spice in short supply, at Christmas cakes and puddings were particularly problematic. This recipe was originally called 'Christmas cake for the children'. Huge efforts were made to guarantee children still had fun at Christmas. If it seems unfair that their parents would miss out, fear not. The cake is pretty good, being both moist and satisfyingly dense if, by modern standards, a little worthy. Admittedly, for those who had enjoyed pre-war Christmas cakes it would probably have tasted more of disappointment.

Original recipe:
½lb flour – 6oz fine sugar – ¾ tsp baking soda – 4 tablespoons treacle – 3oz cleaned currants – ½ tsp ground cloves – 6oz margarine – 1 cup sieved stewed apples – 1 tablespoon warm water – 3oz chopped, stoned raisins – pinch of salt – ¾ tsp ground cinnamon – pinch of grated nutmeg

Beat the margarine to a cream in a basin. Stir in the sugar by degrees, and beat till fluffy. Dissolve soda in the water, mix with apples, and add to sugar and fat. Add treacle. If liked, use half treacle and half golden syrup or clear honey. Sift the flour with

the salt, and spices, then stir in the prepared fruit. Add to the wet
mixture. Stir lightly till well blended. Bake in a greased loaf tin
for 40 minutes in a rather slow oven.

Makes one small cake, using a 450g/1lb loaf tin
170g/6oz butter (or margarine)
170g/6oz caster sugar
½ tsp bicarbonate of soda, dissolved in 1 tbsp warm water
225g/8oz unsweetened apple purée
2 tbsp black treacle
2 tbsp golden syrup
225g/8oz wholemeal flour
85g/3oz currants
85g/3oz raisins
½ tsp ground cloves
¾ tsp ground cinnamon
Pinch of nutmeg
Pinch of salt

Cream the butter and sugar. Mix the bicarb with the apple
puree and beat in. Add the treacle and syrup along with
1 tablespoon of flour to stop it curdling, then mix in the dried
fruit. Sift the flour (this lightens it). Add the spices and salt
and then fold in the flour (if you were left with a load of bran
in the bottom of your sieve, put that in first and mix briefly
before folding in the rest). Bake in a greased loaf tin for
around 1½ hours at 150°C/300°F. The cake should be solid
to the touch, and a skewer should come out clean. Leave in

the tin to cool for 30 minutes before turning out gently to cool completely. Craig suggests icing it and decorating it with polar bears, silver balls or quartered pink marshmallows.

Snacks and titbits

S nacking, in general, isn't socially acceptable – except at Christmas, when it suddenly is. Biscuits and chocolates, dried fruit and nuts, sugar mice and salty things in packets fill the shelves of many a festive larder. The snack market has boomed since the 1950s, and though many of the things which come into the category have been around since the nineteenth century, it is only recently they've been eaten with quite such gay abandon.

Very few snack foods are or were specific to Christmas. In mid- to late-nineteenth-century Derbyshire there was black-ball, described as 'a toffy made at Christmas Day', and which seems to have been a spiced toffee particularly beloved of children. Then there were Norfolk biffins, which were a variety of apple (the Norfolk beefing), dried out slowly in a cool oven until shrivelled and sweet and sold as snack foods from street vendors in London.

Both of these were forgotten by the twentieth century.

Mass-market titbits took over, and, while none of the foods themselves were made only for Christmas, the way they were marketed could make them highly seasonal. Brightly coloured tins for mass-manufactured biscuits were a phenomenon of the late nineteenth century, marketed particularly ferociously at Christmas as being ideal for gifts. Advances in lithographic printing along with the shaping and moulding of tins meant that companies such as Huntley & Palmers or Peek Freans became known for ever more exciting designs. The Huntley & Palmers Christmas range for 1908 included a satchel, a sylvan vase and an ornate casket with ostriches on. By 1925 the discerning biscuit-buyer could opt for a motor van, a train engine, attaché case or windmill.[118] As chocolate confectionery became mass market, with launches such as Quality Street (1936) and Rose's (1938), chocolates, too, were marketed in collectable tins.

Chocolates were, as with biscuits, part of the routine of mealtimes as much as they were casual pick-me-ups. Biscuits went with tea, while chocolate featured at dinner, as part of dessert. Terry's of York made this link explicit in 1926 with the launch of the 'dessert chocolate apple', followed, a decade later, by the chocolate orange. Both were presented in suitably upmarket packaging. However, as the meaning of dessert changed, chocolates became a more general food. The chocolate orange morphed into a Christmas treat, with Terry's playing up the association of oranges with Christmas (the fresh fruit is at its best in the winter) and investing heavily in Christmas advertising. As a result, it became a standard stocking filler, spawning a range of ever-more alarming spin-offs, along with, predictably, Christmas pudding and trifle recipes.

Elsewhere in Northern Europe there were biscuits such as *Kipferl* or *Lebkuchen*, which also influenced American traditions, but never truly caught on in the UK. Even when books solely covering Christmas recipes started to be published, causing authors to look desperately around for dishes beyond the obvious, recipes which could be classed as snacks were centred on shortbread, home-made chocolate truffles, and ingenious ways to use up marzipan. Sections on home-made sweets which appeared in books were intended as much for gift-giving and occupying bored children as they were for serious snacking in the modern sense.

Things got slightly more serious when cocktail parties started to become fashionable, often recycling earlier hors d'oeuvres ideas (themselves a twist on Edwardian savouries, served after the meal along with dessert as a way to cleanse the palate). Frances Carmichael's 1949 list of 'extras for the dinner table' included dried fruit, devilled nuts, marrons glacés, olives, small pickled onions and Turkish delight. 'Most of us like to have on the table small dishes of appetisers that can be nibbled between courses, and home-made sweet-meats,' she declared.[119] It was slightly optimistic, given that rationing was still in force. Meals were smaller then – most of us can barely cope with the ever-increasing spread around the main course these days, let alone wield a cocktail stick in the direction of a cream-cheese-filled prune.

BLACKBALL

Based on accounts of the time plus toffee recipe in Mrs E. W. Kirk, 1929, *Tried Favourites*.[120]

This Derbyshire Christmas speciality is tricky to fathom out. Most descriptions run along the lines of 'the famous blackball – a compound of treacle, sugar, butter and ginger, boiled to a thick syrup which hardened in cooling'.[121] There are no definite recipes, though, just descriptions, often nostalgic or merely observed and a little shaky. However, it is clear that it was made at home, not shop-bought as a lot of sugar confectionery was. It was sticky enough to get stuck in small children's pockets in church, occasioning 'an accusing finger' from the parson, but hard enough to cut into shapes, roll or mould. It predates the invention of golden syrup, and so was probably akin to modern-day bonfire toffee (treacle toffee), with the addition of ground or pounded dried ginger. This version is based on a 1920s recipe for toffee and I've used candied stem ginger instead of dried because I like it. You can add other spices as you fancy.

Original recipe:
1lb sugar, 1lb treacle or syrup, ¼lb butter, a few almonds, a little more than two tablespoons vinegar. Boil over a brisk fire for 20 minutes, stirring all the time.

Makes 24 pieces, 4cm square(ish)
110g/4oz black treacle
110g/4oz brown sugar
25g/1oz butter
1 tbsp finely minced stem ginger (in syrup) – you can also
    use crystallised ginger
1 tsp vinegar

Put everything into a heavy-bottomed saucepan and heat gently until the ingredients are melted. Stir to combine. Increase the heat and boil until the mixture reaches hard crack (150°C/300°F). Pour on to a lightly greased baking sheet (or use a silicon baking mat) and allow to cool enough to handle. For shapes, cool until it is almost set and then score with a greased, sharp knife, or for balls, roll the toffee into balls while it is still soft enough to be malleable. Be careful not to burn yourself, though.

ANOTHER CHRISTMAS COOKEY

Amelia Simmons, 1796, *American Cookery*[122]

American Cookery was the first recipe book to be written by an American author for an American audience, and as such was an important marker for the newly independent country. It includes recipes for native ingredients such as pumpkin and turkey, as well as bringing together some of the many European influences from immigrants to the country. This Dutch-influenced cookey (the name cookey comes from the Dutch) is very like seventeenth-century dessert biscuits, intended for dipping in wine. They make excellent tree ornaments, as they benefit from keeping.

Original recipe:
To three pound flour, sprinkle a tea cup of fine powdered coriander seed, rub in one pound butter, and one and half pound sugar, dissolve three teaspoonfuls of pearl ash in a tea cup of milk, kneed all together well, roll three quarters of an inch thick, and cut or stamp into shape and size you please, bake slowly fifteen or twenty minutes; tho' hard and dry at first, if put into an earthen pot, and dry cellar, or damp room, they will be finer, softer and better when six months old.

Makes around 30 × 5cm/2 inch biscuits
55g/2oz butter
170g/6oz flour, plus extra for dusting

75g/3oz golden caster sugar
10g/½oz ground coriander
Generous pinch of baking powder
60ml/2½fl oz milk
2 egg yolks, plus a splash of milk and a pinch of salt, to
   glaze

Crumb the butter into the flour, add the sugar and coriander
and mix well. Dissolve the baking powder in the milk and add
to the mixture. Knead by hand or in a stand mixer until it
forms a robust, not sticky, dough.

Flour a work surface, and roll out the dough to around
1cm/just under ½ inch thick. Stamp out biscuits using whatever cutter you fancy. Bake at 180°C/350°F for 25–30
minutes, until pale brown and rock hard.

While they are baking, make an egg wash by whisking the
egg yolks with a splash of milk and a pinch of salt (you can
use icing sugar instead, but the biscuits are fairly sweet
already). When the biscuits are done, remove them from the
oven and brush all over the top with the egg wash. Return
them to the oven for 1 minute. Remove, cool slightly, and
repeat. Now flip them over and glaze the bottoms.

The biscuits can be eaten straight away, in which case they
benefit from dunking or you risk your teeth breaking.
However, Simmons recommends keeping them for up to six
months, during which time they will soften. Realistically a
month or so is plenty. (Keep in a cool, dry place.)

Leftovers

The Boxing Day leftover feast is as much a part of many people's Christmas as Christmas dinner itself. Turkey curry is a mainstay, but a terribly English smorgasbord of cold cuts pepped up with Christmas chutney is hardly a rarity. It is, perhaps, the one time of the year when leftovers are celebrated, rather than regarded as sad sloppy seconds.

Attitudes have changed. With meat at a premium, leftovers were previously an important part of household meal planning. In wealthy households anything uneaten from the top tables was fair game for the servants. Both ideal and real menus from houses with staff show that by the Victorian period, at least, they were integrated into menus, rather than left for a free-for-all. *Cre-Fydd's Family Fare*, from 1865, includes the usual roast beef, boiled fowl and plum pudding on its Christmas Day menu for the family, along with roast goose and plum pudding for the servants. On the 26th upstairs are on cold beef, and minced fowl, and on the 27th, beef in 'acid sauce' and croquettes of fowl (essentially breadcrumbed meatballs made with minced cooked meat). Downstairs finish up their own goose and then move on to the beef joint which is still hanging around from upstairs. Nearly a century later, staff menus from the household of Winston Churchill include numerous references such as '2 pieces of fish from dining room luncheon'.[123] Until the Second World War, in the richest households, anything still left would be parcelled up to be distributed to the poor.

However, not every establishment had staff, and many of those that did only employed one or two young girls. By the Victorian era 'cold meat cookery' had become an established section in recipe books. The Georgians had relied on hashes, which were usually thick slices of meat reheated gently in a strongly savoury gravy, enhanced with mushroom catsup (or ketchup – a condiment not unlike Worcestershire sauce), anchovies or lemon. Potted meat was also popular, seasoned with mace, pepper and brandy, and topped with clarified butter. Or there were salads or jellied meats, such as the evocatively named 'to congeal a turkey' from 1661.[124] By the 1860s hash was becoming a dirty word, the dish name adapted to mean reheated ideas, and the dish itself associated with unimaginative cookery.

Beef was easy to deal with, served cold for breakfast or in sandwiches. Further down the line it could be added to toad-in-the-hole or Irish stew. Poultry was harder. The main Victorian solution was to mince it, mix it with butter, flour and egg, shape it, breadcrumb it and fry it. Rissoles, croquettes and turkey cutlets were all based on this principle (one book suggested adding a piece of pasta at the pointy end of the latter, to resemble a bone, which the diner then presumably removed). Blanquettes and stews were common as well, including *à la Bretonne* (it sounded better in French), which was browned onions, haricot beans and gravy. By the 1870s leftover cookery was termed 'réchauffé' or 'second dressing', just to add a bit of glamour to proceedings. Visual flair was important, and, as ever, moulds were pressed into service, particularly for making 'meat shape'. Recipes for this are as ghastly as they sound; meat, egg, suet and rather minimal seasoning all steamed in a mould and turned out. One variation (which at least includes curry powder), instructs the cook to make it in a decorative ring mould, the centre then filled with cold boiled vegetables covered in salad dressing.

There were solutions proposed, as well, for the various extras – cold potatoes could be used for pastry, or fried in slices or cakes (to be hollowed out and stuffed with a hash, in one case). Absolutely anything could be devilled, by dint of adding cayenne, mustard and relishes and frying it – one writer listed 'bones, biscuits, meat and fish'.[125] Cooked vegetables (plus apple and cucumber) formed the basis for an excellent vegetable curry for Katherine Mellish in 1901.[126] And fried sliced plum pudding was a standard sweet leading up to the New Year.

It wasn't until the twentieth century that Christmas leftovers became a cause for celebration, linked in part to the codification of Christmas dinner and subsequent abandonment of many of its foods at any other time of the year. Curries, in vogue for using up cold meat since the mid-nineteenth century (earlier recipes used fresh meat), were perennially popular, but there were other, more esoteric suggestions from writers keen to showcase their inventiveness. Style did sometimes triumph over substance. Fanny Cradock covered leftovers in 1967's *Problem Cooking*, adhering firmly to the belief that a good name is always a solid start. Hence 'Pitt-y-pana', made of minced cold meat, stale breadcrumbs and cold cooked potato, all fried with up with an onion, piled in a bowl and served with an egg yolk on the half shell pressed into the centre. The diner mixed the yolk into the rest, and apparently it cooked and made a sauce at the same time. She also suggested 'sad, stale' sandwiches could be battered and deep-fried and served with deep-fried sprouts, which sounds a tad more toothsome.

The euphoria of the post-war culinary scene didn't always lead to such novelties, though. Marguerite Patten opted for a much more conservative turkey casserole with savoury dumplings or a quickly made pie with potato crust. Still, a heap of leftovers does seem to unleash something within some writers. Readers of *Microwave Know-How* in 1985 would learn how to make an Eastern-spiced turkey, whose main requirements were peppers, onions, two tins of tomatoes and a tin of 'mango, apricot or peach slices, drained'. The same year, *Good Housekeeping*'s rather token section on Boxing Day sustenance in their 'Cooking for Christmas' book included turkey, pineapple and pasta salad, which starts as you'd expect, before veering alarmingly off to include horseradish, tomato puree, celery – and a topping of salted peanuts.[127] In for a few leftovers, in for the whole lot.

BANANA PLUM PUDDING

Elizabeth Craig, 1962, *Banana Dishes*[128]

There are almost as many plum pudding recipes as there are recipe books: it is such a British staple that nearly every author has had a crack at one. For an excellent, conventional pudding, Eliza Acton's Author's Christmas pudding is hard to beat, but for the purposes of this book I tried a lot of them (avoid at all costs the wartime ones). However, while lots were excellent, for something slightly different this banana-y riff on the theme is very good fun. It is also pure 1960s — earlier banana books (*Many Ways with Bananas*, for example, from 1900) tended towards Charlottes and fools, fritters and preserves, whereas Craig's suggestions are gloriously bonkers from a modern perspective. Note that even as late as 1962, cooks are still advised to stone their own raisins. The instructions are exact on the ingredients, but assume the cook knows exactly what to do with a pudding cloth.

Original recipe

4oz cleaned currants, 4oz cleaned sultanas, 6oz raisins, 7oz shredded suet, 4oz flour, 1 teaspoon ground ginger, 4oz chopped candied peel, 1oz blanched almonds, 1 tablespoon ground almonds, 4oz caster sugar, 4 peeled bananas, 2 beaten eggs, ¼ pt milk. Mix currants and sultanas. Stone and chop raisins and add. Mix suet, flour and ginger. Add peel. Chop and add almonds. Stir into flour. Add prepared fruit, ground almonds and sugar.

Peel and slice bananas thinly. Stir into mixture. Stir eggs into
milk. Make hollow in centre of fruit mixture. Pour in liquid and
stir until thoroughly mixed. Pack into a well-greased pudding
basin to within an inch of top. Cover with greased paper, then
with floured pudding cloth. Tie securely. Place in saucepan. Add
boiling water to half-way up the sides. Steam for about 6 hours.
Unmould onto heated platter. Decorate with a sprig of holly.
Sprinkle with heated brandy, rum or whisky and set a match to it.
Serve with banana sauce.

Makes 1 pudding (best in a 900ml / 1½ pint mould, but will just
fit in a 600ml / 1 pint one)
55g / 2oz each currants, sultanas, candied peel, caster sugar
    and flour
85g / 3oz raisins – chopped in half if very large
100g / 3½oz suet
14g / ½oz chopped almonds
1 heaped tsp ground almonds
1 level tsp ground ginger
2 bananas
75ml / 2½floz full-fat milk
1 lightly beaten egg

Mix all the dry ingredients. Chop or slice the bananas and add
them, followed by the milk and egg. Mix well. Grease a basin
or mould (it's the 1960s, so a fluted ceramic number would be
entirely appropriate), and pour in the mixture. Lay a disc of
greased baking parchment on top, and tie over a cloth or foil.

If using a cloth, wet it, squeeze it out and flour lightly. Either way, put a fold in the cloth or foil to allow for expansion. Tie firmly in place (you can just scrunch if foil), and place on a saucer or small trivet in a saucepan of boiling water. The water should be just over halfway up the bowl. Put a lid on the pan and boil for 6 hours, checking regularly in case it boils dry.

The recipe is intended to be boiled and served straight away, but it can also be made a couple of weeks in advance and reheated, in which case store it in a clean cloth somewhere cool and dry. Craig suggests a sauce of maple syrup and mashed banana, but this may be a step too far.

A MICROWAVE CHRISTMAS (1985)

Marshall Cavendish, *Microwave Know-How*[129]

Turkey with apple and chestnut stuffing

Carrot and coriander stuffing ring

Roast potatoes

Brussels sprouts and almonds

Peas and fennel

Cranberry sauce

Bread sauce

Gravy

Christmas pudding with brandy butter

Bring back the twelfth cake

Christmas cake is a conundrum. As fabulous as it is, it can be hard to place. When, exactly, is the appropriate time to eat it? On Christmas Day, when we're already replete? Boxing Day, as a lift from leftovers? When we have guests? But then which ones do we like enough to spare a piece, and does it look rude if it has already been cut? Or should we simply eat it all Christmas, whenever needed, and preferably with cheese? (This last is a northern habit, and excellent beyond all measure.)

There is a simpler solution. For around 300 years the cake we associate with Christmas was, for many people, not about Christmas at all, but an even more uproarious and highly specific celebration: that of the Epiphany, Twelfth Night, celebrated in Britain on January 6th.

Twelfth Night signals the end of old Twelve Days, the closing of the festive season, and a day therefore made for seeing off Christmas in style. Associated in the Christian calendar with the three kings, by the time its various rituals started to be written about in the fifteenth century, it was already one of the high points of the season. As shenanigans based on social upheaval became more muted, it remained the one day when such elements still came to the fore, and by the early seventeenth century it had become established as the night for private parties centred on selecting a temporary king through the medium of cake.

Celebratory cakes have a long history, but the history of the twelfth cake is linked to one particular form: the rich fruit cake. These started life in the medieval period as spiced and fruited breads, which gained in popularity until, inevitably, the Tudor and early Stuart authorities decided to regulate them. Various orders were issued in various towns attempting to limit the sale of spice cakes and buns to Christmas, Easter and funerals.[130] They didn't work. Bakers and, later, confectioners, happily provided cakes which were beyond the reach of most of their clientele through simple practicality (i.e. lack of ovens, time and ingredients). While there were simple, small spiced breads, such as cross buns (generally offered hot, hence the later name), for a really good party something more was required. By the seventeenth century printed and manuscript books frequently contain recipes for 'plum cake' or 'great cake'. Surviving recipes indicate that they could be monsters: one 1653 recipe uses 56lb (25.4kg) of flour along with 8lb (3.6kg) of currants.[131] Yeast-risen, with a spice blend heavy on mace, cinnamon and nutmeg, as was characteristic of the time, the fruit content was low in early recipes, but increased over the next 200 years. Candied peel and other fruit also played a larger role in later cakes.

Cakes like this were eaten at any celebration, but at Twelfth Night they were used as part of what became a very particular custom. In 1676 Henry Teonge, a naval chaplain, recounted 'we had much mirth on board, for we had a great cake made, in which was put a bean for the king, a pea for the queen, a clove for the knave, a forked stick for the cuckold, a rag for the slut. The cake was cut into several pieces in the great cabin, and all put into a napkin, out of which everyone took his piece, as out of a lottery; then each piece broken to see what was in it, which caused much laughter.'[132] At its most basic twelfth cake was a fruit cake, of reasonable size, with a dried bean hidden within it, sometimes joined by a pea. Whoever found the bean in their slice was the king; the pea denoted the queen. The first explicit mention of the ceremony in this form comes from 1592, but the idea of a bean king was already established, and the phrase was in use as one of mockery. The cake wasn't yet always called twelfth cake; various names swirled around, and are hard to pin down, but they included bean cake, king cake and baby cake.

By the time Teonge was enjoying his cake, the fun of allotting characters had progressed to include a range of other equally mocking stereotypes. Pepys, another twelfth cake fan, greatly enjoyed rigging the drawing of the tokens so that a friend of his, under investigation for fraud, found the clove. It worked only because it was a private joke. Teonge's, too, was a cake with a restricted audience – not the ordinary sailors, but the officers, and indeed twelfth cake seems to have remained upper-class for a long time. It also seems to have been a largely urban phenomenon. The first mention of it in the context of a recipe is from 1768, when James Jenks noted that his 'rich cake' 'is called a Twelfth Cake at London'. His recipe, which is a reworked and garbled version of one of Hannah Glasse's, starts with 6lb (2.7kg) of butter worked with 3lb (1.7kg) of sugar, the same of almonds, plus 4lb (1.8kg) of eggs and flour and a pint (568ml) of brandy and sack. The spice mixture now includes ginger and cloves along with the mace, cinnamon and nutmeg, 7lb (3.2kg) of currants and as much candied peel 'as may be thought convenient'.[133] By now, the yeast-risen cakes of earlier eras were yielding to egg-based mixtures, with far more fruit and sugar. Britain's colonisation of the West Indies and America, and exploitation of slave labour, meant that sugar, while still expensive, was not the luxury it had been, and the range and affordability of sweet goods boomed. Almond paste (marzipan) and icing came in around the same time, the latter initially meringue-like, needing baking to dry.

Choosing the bean king was changing, too. Back in the 1660s Pepys complained that there was such a scrum over the cake that the tokens got lost and the cake was destroyed. By the end of that century a new ritual was developing, whereby the characters were simply written on paper, and picked from a hat. Canny printers recognised an opportunity, and by the end of the eighteenth century the would-be reveller could buy a pack of Twelfth Night characters, refreshed every year and based on society figures or stock characters. Each character came with a riddle or joke, thus in 1844, Park's Twelfth Night characters included Sir Oliver Ogle, with the question 'Why is a lover like a gooseberry?' ('Because he is easily made a fool of'). The cakes themselves were also becoming ever more outlandish. Most depictions of twelfth cakes show them fairly simply adorned, generally with a crown and, by the nineteenth century, applied decoration made in pastillage and moulded. But as their popularity grew, and price decreased, there was, briefly, a real cult around them. *Punch* magazine labelled Twelfth Night 'all cakes day'.

They peaked in the decades around 1830, when according to Willian Hone, 'in London, with every pastrycook in the city, and at the west end of the town, it is "high change" on Twelfth-day. From the taking down of the shutters in the morning, he, and his men, with additional assistants, male and female, are fully occupied by attending to the dressing out of the window, executing orders of the day before, receiving fresh ones, or supplying the wants of chance customers. Before dusk the important arrangement of the window is completed. Then the gas is turned on, with supernumerary argand-lamps and manifold wax-lights, to illuminate countless cakes of all prices and dimensions, that stand in rows and piles on the counters and sideboards, and in the windows. The richest in flavour and heaviest in weight and price are placed on large and massy salvers; one, enormously superior to the rest in size, is the chief object of curiosity; and all are decorated with all imaginable images of things animate and inanimate. Stars, castles, kings, cottages, dragons, trees, fish, palaces, cats, dogs, churches, lions, milk-maids, knights, serpents, and innumerable other forms in snow-white confectionary, painted with variegated colours, glitter by "excess of light" from mirrors against the walls festooned with artificial "wonders of Flora". This "paradise of dainty devices", is crowded by successive and successful desirers of the seasonable delicacies, while alternate tapping of hammers and peals of laughters, from the throng surrounding the house, excite smiles from the inmates.'[134]

The royal twelfth cakes were particularly glorious, and the Queen maintained the habit until her death in 1901. That of 1849 was described – and pictured – in the *Illustrated London News*. Topped with sugarpaste figures having a bucolic *déjeuner sur l'herbe*, it was bordered with gold paper cut into strips which would have waved pleasingly in the draught that blew around the corridors of Windsor Castle. But just a few years later there were signs that its popularity, which seems never to have really become established outside London, was waning.

While fruit cake could be made at home, as twelfth cake it was more often the province of the caterer because of the need for decoration. Even where the basic cake was made in-house, the ornaments were bought in. One 1830s recipe states quite simply that a twelfth cake is to be prepared 'as for bride cake, plum cake or pound cake', then iced and 'lay on your ornaments while the icing is wet, get them from the confectioner'.[135] But this was the heyday of food adulteration, or at least of growing public consciousness of it. In 1851 *Punch* decried 'the confectioner-Imp, who paints Twelfth Cakes with emerald green (a beautiful change for coppers, in an arsenite development) and – especially in holiday-times – plays Herod among the innocents'.[136] The colourful gaudiness of some cakes also offended. Twelfth cake just wasn't exclusive any more. Even in the 1760s James Boswell wrote happily of strolling round London eating 'penny twelfth cakes at every shop where I could get it', and by the 1840s they were available for every budget. Charles Dickens, who was used to elaborate cakes from London's leading confectioners, sniffily described one up for raffle in *The Mystery of Edwin Drood* as 'such a very poor little Twelfth cake, that one would rather call it a Twenty-fourth cake, or a Forty-eighth cake'.[137]

Then there was the inexorable expansion of Christmas to encompass anything previously more generally seasonal. In Scotland, rich fruit cakes were eaten at Hogmanay, with similar scenes of delight and anticipation outside confectioners' windows as were the case for English Twelfth Night. Christmas was still in a distant second place to Hogmanay, and the Scottish Black bun, as it became known towards the end of the century, hung on as a New Year treat. In England, though, twelfth cake started giving way to Christmas cake; still a plum cake, still heavy and still iced. It was influenced by changing habits elsewhere. The name 'Christmas cake' was recorded in New Zealand and Australia before it was taken up by the British at home, a reflection, perhaps, of the failure of twelfth cake to really catch on outside the upper classes or in

London: those seeking new lives on the other side of the globe were often rural farmers, who were incentivised with free or assisted passages.

But there were differences. Christmas cake was a domestic cake. It was easy to make at home, without professional help, and it inevitably lacked the exuberance of its fruity cousin. Contemporary illustrations show muted decoration and basic icing. Piping techniques came in around the mid-nineteenth century, for those who had the time or staff, with measured swirls and symmetrical precision. Milkmaids and starfish were replaced with piped writing. Divorced from Twelfth Night, and in the new atmosphere of the family-friendly Christmas, there was no point in playing games with scurrilous characters and faintly smutty rhymes. The groan-inducing jokes of the Twelfth Night cards and the paper crowns worn by the bean king didn't disappear completely. Instead they were reborn inside the brilliantly named 'bangs of expectation', sadly renamed as crackers not long after. By the end of the century the bean had been reborn too, as it was recast as a sixpence for luck and started to appear inside the Christmas pudding.

Christmas cake was staid, and sensible, and, like so many elements of the English Christmas, became a global success. British immigrants to Australia, Canada and New Zealand continued to eat it, adapting it to climate and culture, making it a long-lasting part of Commonwealth Christmases. Others took it to America, but it never gained widespread acceptance. Rich, hefty fruit cake was now very British, despite its pan-European roots. Most other European countries had fruited breads or cakes associated with Christmas, including panettone and stollen, but they were lighter, and generally un-iced. Even in 1844 Dickens' annual twelfth cake treat, sent to him that year in Genoa, had bewildered the Swiss confectioners to whom he sent it for some judicious mending, and attracted a crowd of incredulous locals who came to stare at it in the window. By 1901 rich fruit cake was openly branded as one of the national specialities.

The twentieth century was one of steady domestication. Christmas cakes got smaller and sweeter. Recipes changed slowly, though, reflecting a deep-seated belief in tradition and a desire for continuity. Fruit cake doesn't even make the top ten in polls of Britons' top cakes: if it's only made once a year it's hardly going to be at the forefront of change. However, by the 1950s most recipes included baking powder along with the eggs, while the variety of fruit had expanded – 'Granny's Christmas Cake' in Frances Carmichael's 1949 *Christmas Cooking* includes currants, raisins, sultanas, candied peel, glacé cherries, glacé pineapple and preserved ginger. Taken with the margarine, it's a rather unlikely combination for Carmichael's actual Granny to have cooked. But she also included a 'Christmas Yeast Cake', a throwback, really, to her great-great-Granny's time. Giving Christmas cakes provenance (real or not) was common. From the 1960s, Isobel Barnett's superlative 'Aunt Margaret's Christmas Cake' is pretty standard: 12oz each of brown sugar and butter, 2 tablespoons of treacle, 1lb flour, nearly 3lb of fruit, almonds, brandy and generic 'spice'. An alternative was to use a pound cake as a base – equal amounts of flour, butter, sugar and eggs – varying the fruit and spice according to the writer. They were universally intended to be made at home, decorated simply, in an era where few people now had cooks.

By the 1980s the perplexing habit of 'feeding the cake' had started creep in. It was (and is) entirely unnecessary, for most cakes happily kept for months wrapped in paper or in a cake tin, which was the standard advice. Christmas cakes were intended to be marzipanned and iced, further sealing them. There were a few published recipes from the 1920s for rich fruit cakes where alcohol was poured over them when hot, and recipes for other cakes, more likely to go stale, which were revitalised with spirits (plus the whole category of alcohol-imbibed cakes such as babas).[138] In 1971 Delia Smith advised buying a cake and pimping it by feeding it with brandy – but this was very much a cheat for a shop-bought cake.[139] Katie Stewart's 1983 directions remained the norm: 'allow to cool in the tin for 30 minutes, then turn out and leave for 24 hours. Wrap in kitchen foil and store for at least 1 week or up to a month.' Her cake was then finished with almond paste and icing.[140] A generation later, however, the idea had been popularised. Smith, by now regarded as a culinary icon, on whose word hitherto obscure ingredients would fly from the supermarket shelves, had adapted it for her home-made Christmas cake, and other authors quickly followed. Despite the extra time and thought required, it was a gentle way to lead up to Christmas. For some, it became as

much a ritual for some as poking a bean into the batter had
been for others 300 years before.

Other countries still have twelfth cakes – in France the
ceramic token found inside the galette or gateau des rois is
still called the *fève*, meaning dried bean. The uproarious traditions of the Twelfth Night party have successfully been
tamed, made into a celebration suitable for children and
adults alike. Maybe instead of packing up the decorations
well before the 6th of January, we should reinvent our own
twelfth cake for the twenty-first century, and enjoy one, last,
resounding huzzah, before the inevitable return to sensible
eating, work and another new year.

TWELFTH CAKE

John Mollard, 1803, *The Art of Cookery*[141]

The first published recipe to be explicitly called Twelfth Cake, this is essentially a yeast-risen fruit cake of the seventeenth- and eighteenth-century type, more often called plum cake, rich cake, or great cake in the past. It was being eclipsed by more modern versions with eggs in place of the yeast even by the time it was published. If you want to add in a dried bean and pea, go for it, though my advice would be to wrap them in foil so they are easily spotted. Alternatively, push a bean and pea up into the cake from the bottom after it is baked – they run less of a risk of disintegrating slightly and getting eaten by an eager party-goer. This cake is particularly excellent spread with butter or as an accompaniment to cheese. Unlike rich fruit cake, it isn't a keeper, and will go stale after about a week (but does then make excellent trifle or bread and butter pudding).

Original recipe:
Take seven pounds of flour, make a cavity in the centre, set a sponge with a gill and a half of yeast and a little warm milk; then put round it one pound of fresh butter broke into small lumps, one pound and a quarter of sifted sugar, four pounds and a half of currants washed and picked, half an ounce of sifted cinnamon, a quarter of an ounce of pounded cloves, mace, and nutmeg mixed, sliced candied orange or lemon peel and citron. When the sponge is risen, mix all the ingredients together with a

little warm milk; let the hoops be well papered and buttered, then fill them with the mixture and bake them, and when nearly cold ice them over with sugar prepared for that purpose as per receipt; or they may be plain.

Makes one 22cm/9 inch cake
400ml milk
2 sachets/14g of dried yeast
800g/1lb 12oz flour
115g/4oz butter, at room temperature
510g/1lb 2oz currants
100g/4oz candied peel
1 tsp ground cinnamon
¼ tsp each ground cloves, nutmeg, mace
140g/5oz caster sugar
15g salt

Heat 100ml of milk until lukewarm and add the yeast. Stir to mix. Make a well in the centre of the flour and pour in the yeast mixture. Scatter flour from around the edges over the liquid, enough to cover it. Cover the bowl with a clean tea-towel and leave for between 30 minutes and 2 hours, until the yeast mixture bubbles through the flour. Gently mix in more flour from around the edges to form a paste in the middle and leave for a further 30 minutes. You can also leave it overnight if you need to.

Cut the butter into small chunks and dot around the edges of the bowl. Add the fruit, spice, sugar and salt, together with the remaining milk. Mix, either by hand or in a mixer, then knead for 20 minutes if by hand, or 10 minutes if in a mixer. Cover and leave to prove for 2–3 hours, until it is spongy – a finger pushed gently into the dough should leave a dimple which gradually springs back. Don't worry if it does not rise very much: although this is a yeasted mixture, it doesn't behave quite like bread as the weight of fruit tends to curb its enthusiasm.

Grease a 22cm/9 inch springform cake tin, and line the bottom and sides with several layers of baking parchment. Add the dough, and leave for a further 20–30 minutes before baking at 160°C/325°F for 1 hour 30 minutes to 1 hour 45 minutes. A digital probe will read 94°C when it is done – you can also use a knife or skewer to test for doneness as you would with a conventional cake.

Leave to cool. Mollard suggests you can serve it plain, or iced, in which case he is quite keen on red icing. However, since the result is more like bread than cake, I would err towards leaving it un-iced.

Post-war and beyond:
Christmas in technicolour

The 1950s saw the end of rationing, and was a decade of
recovery and change. For some, it was a time to move
forward, embracing modernity which, in the kitchen, meant
new gadgets and an enthusiasm for convenience foods and
patent mixtures. For others, it was a chance to reclaim the
habits of the past, and, while many women sought to take
advantage of potential domestic shortcuts and refused to be
confined to the home, others gladly gave up their war work
and returned to scrubbing their war-worn sinks.

Domestic service was in decline. Middle-class women
who might have managed a cook-general or char before the
war now found themselves cooking for their families with
little or no outside help. In the introduction to the 1950s *Constance Spry Cookery Book*, Spry reflected on her first meeting
with her co-author, Rosemary Hume: 'little did I realise what
was at stake when I went to see her, for I did not realise, nor

do I think did she, what a big part cookery was to play in the lives of women after the war'.[142] Packet sauces, ready-made puddings and tinned foods came of age, not just in everyday cooking but, increasingly, for Christmas too.

Christmas Day was now the focal point of the season, finally even recognised as a public holiday in Scotland in 1958. The variety seen in pre-war ideal menus lessened even for the rich, who still had staff, but fewer of them. Some turned to foreign labour, employed on short-term contracts due to immigration laws, and then complained that the Austrian teenagers in their kitchens struggled to turn out a decent plum pudding.

Smaller households and limited cooks meant that one joint was now the norm, with three or four sides. As farming technology changed, and seasonality, especially in meat, became a thing of the past, that joint was now overwhelmingly likely to be chicken or turkey, which, from the 1970s, could be bought frozen, bred and killed at a time convenient to farmers, and was cheaper than ever before. D. D. Cottingham Taylor's recommended dinner for a family on a tight budget in the early 1950s was roast turkey, chestnut stuffing, sausages, bread sauce, gravy, mashed or chip potatoes, Brussels sprouts, Christmas pudding and brandy sauce. Cold turkey, salad, mince pies and cheese followed as a light supper.[143] Thirty years later the *Coventry Evening Telegraph* had added a starter – the classic 1970s melon in brandy – but otherwise the menu merely swapped croquette and roast potatoes for the mash, and added braised celery and peas.

The stuffing was generic, no flavour specified. Readers were exhorted to plan well ahead 'so that mum can get to grips with the sherry and parcel-opening on Christmas morning instead of standing over a hot stove'. Most of the suggested planning involved the must-have gadget of the age – the chest freezer.[144]

The core of the meal, then, was set, crossing classes, regions and assumed to be universal in popular culture. There was, nevertheless, resistance. Many people still couldn't afford turkey and found it too large. In a reversal of the situation 100 years before, goose was now more expensive than turkey, as it was harder to farm, and so became a good way to show off. Beef still hung on, especially in Ireland, where spiced rolled beef was a seasonal speciality. However, it and ham tended to be brought forward to Christmas Eve or pushed back to Boxing Day. The vegetarian movement was becoming (slightly) more mainstream, though nut roasts were about as good as it got.

Outside the holy triumvirate of turkey, trimmings and Christmas pudding (and mince pies, eaten at an indeterminate point but rarely at dinner), though, there was scope for creativity. Cookery writers, vying to come up with something original, abandoned all thoughts of restraint or, in some cases, sense, and the 1960s and 1970s witnessed a truly splendid outpouring of brightly coloured, fantastically styled dishes. It was nothing new – trompe d'œil foods and incredible concoctions in jelly had long made their appearance on many a celebratory table, but now, in an age of everything in packets, they were accessible to all. There was a lot of food proposed in all the ideal menus though, and it is hard to escape the conclusion that some authors were happy to propose menus to be cooked by one person which, just twenty years before, would not have been attempted without at least the assistance of a daily char.

For much of the year, women, to whom the vast majority of domestic cooking still fell, didn't have time to sculpt penguins out of eggs and olives, or set tealights into cranberry jelly, but, at least in the eyes of magazine commissioners and cookery book writers, Christmas was the one time when they should really make an effort. The pressure to perform, to make one perfect day, was intense. Though some thrived on the chance to build and maintain family-specific culinary rituals, not everyone was in agreement. One 1961 author commented, '"Christmas comes but once a year" – for which many of us tend to mutter "and a good thing too", particularly those of us who are responsible, single-handed, for the cooking side of the festival'.[145]

While the Sunday roast still ruled supreme, and most women would have been able to handle the enhanced version proposed for them at Christmas, not everyone was a skilled or willing cook. Anecdotal evidence suggests the latter view prevailed, and, while the inevitability of hard labour was accepted or embraced, the wilder excesses of the 1970s Christmas pushed by books and magazines rarely made it off the page. Nor was the growing insistence that everything be made from scratch reflected in reality. Cookery books are intrinsically aspirational and, while cookery slowly became ubiquitous on TV, it was watched as much to entertain as to inform.[146]

Outside the sit-down Christmas dinner, change was more visible. At formal meals, this was the age of the heated hostess trolley, but for entertaining the finger buffet made it easier to manage more people than would fit around the average table. The late 1970s Cordon Bleu cookery course proposed a Boxing Day buffet party menu which included ham cornets filled with foie gras and bechamel sauce flavoured with sherry and topped with truffle. In a gesture which would have been familiar to any self-respecting nineteenth-century cook, the garnish was chopped (tinned) aspic. More gelatine and bechamel was used for the decidedly beige egg mousse with devilled sauce which followed. Marguerite Patten also opted for cornets for her festive party fare, in this case bread moulded round cream horn cases and filled with cream cheese. Other visually striking suggestions included grapes and nuts with cheese on sticks, bacon frankfurters and tiny bowls made out of salami, filled with baked beans and potato salad (harder to make than they sound). She also proposed a sandwich gateau: a multi-layered brick of sliced white bread with 'varied sandwich fillings', slathered with mayonnaise and cottage cheese, and with a final instruction to 'garnish gaily'.[147] Dessert options included mincemeat meringue pie and a platter of suitably shaped Christmas biscuits.

Alongside eager exploration of processed foods and modern technology, though, some authors were already looking back to the past. While the renaissance in British food wouldn't hit the mainstream until the 1980s, the quiet awareness that there was much to admire in the past was growing. Even Fanny Cradock published a recipe for 'Escoffier's super Christmas pudding' (not quite the original name) as well as various historically inspired (lethal) drinks.[148] Cradock later came to be a byword for extravagance and over-the-top presentation, but she was wildly popular, and exemplified the post-war desire for colour, texture and fun.

In 1975 her five-part *Fanny Cradock Cooks for Christmas* aired, accompanied with a recipe booklet.[149] The series remains an unalloyed joy, despite Cradock's evident exasperation with performing recipes she'd done every year for decades. In the first episode Cradock pipes stuffing into a turkey (it gushes up her wrists), attacks a goose with a fork (lets out the fat, and lets in the honey baste), and shows the housewives of Britain how to beat their annoying menfolk at carving a chicken with deft use of pair of (disinfected) garden secateurs. In later episodes she does unnecessarily complicated things to get a cannonball-shaped Christmas pudding, hoicks cake mix into a tin with the grace of a cement mixer, and makes a satisfyingly large mincemeat tart (much preferred, apparently, by men) – all in filmy outfits with never a hint of an apron. There's an alarming reliance on green food colouring (mash, brandy butter, glacé cherries). But underneath all the pink-clad silliness, the underlying tension of the post-war Christmas still lurks. Despite declaring that Christmas is 'slave labour for women', and promising quick, easy, ways to address the issues, Cradock is still part of the problem, reinforcing the idea that the pantheon of Christmas dishes is sacrosanct, and that all must ultimately be attempted.

A generation after rationing, Britain was both rediscovering its own food heritage and embracing new flavours. As the new millennium beckoned, Christmas dinner remained poised, as it long had, between nostalgia and modernity, between technological change and deeply held notions of tradition. Cookery writers could exhort and advise all they wanted, but British cooks remained conservative. However, while a dinner in 1980 might have looked the same as that of 1950, underneath it had changed. Piped potato mash might have been a passing phase, but gravy granules, stuffing mixes, custard power and shop-bought mincemeat were now the norm as never before. With women now working and still doing most of the cooking, they were as important as any of the changes wrought in earlier centuries.

'CLASSIC' CHRISTMAS MENU (2019)

Ellie Donnell, *Delicious Magazine*[150]

Nibbles and starters
Blinis with smoked salmon and dill

The main event
Classic (and easy) Christmas turkey
Perfect roast potatoes
Brussels sprouts and bacon
Turkey gravy
Pigs in blankets
Chestnut and pork stuffing
Balsamic and brown sugar roast carrots and parsnips

The pudding
Traditional Christmas pudding
or
Yule log

A post-prandial postscript

I n the back of the best-selling *Delia Smith's Christmas*, published in 1990, the uncertain cook could find a handy guide
to 'the last 36 hours'. Although Smith gave a wide range of
recipes in the rest of the book, this section cut to the chase.
Early morning on Christmas Eve was for last-minute food
shopping; important to be back for mid-morning when the
turkey would arrive. The rest of the day was spent preparing
vegetables, making trifle, stuffing, sauces, and ensuring the
fridge was well-stocked with wine. A scheduled break to
listen to carols was allowed – while baking mince pies. On
Christmas Day itself, she suggested 7.45am as a good time to
preheat the oven, with a break just before 9am to 'help the
kids unwrap their presents, have a coffee or tidy the house'.
Later came steaming the pudding, roasting sausages, potatoes
and parsnips, making gravy and finally cooking the sprouts.[151]

Christmas dinner is full of tension. It is a deeply significant occasion through which to build and maintain family

connections by the construction of rituals individual to each family. Men and women both play a role in this. Surveys show that men are more likely to be traditionalist, clinging to the customs of their own upbringing and insistent that things remain the same, year on year. Women, meanwhile, are more recognisant of the work involved, mainly because they still do most of it. Smith was very careful not to assign a gender to her 'frazzled' cook, or to the carver who is summoned towards the end, but implicit within her, and most other Christmas books, is the notion that the cook is female. It remains true that, in most households, this assumption is correct. This isn't to suggest that men don't play an active role in Christmas cookery, or that women are poor, put-upon creatures who should be pitied and plied with gin in recompense. But there is still more pressure on women than on men to produce the 'perfect' Christmas dinner and, in doing so, lay down happy memories for the future while reinforcing those of the past.

There may be people for whom Delia Smith's timetable is perfect. But for the generation who came of age after the millennium it strikes fear into the heart. Christmas dinner is not immutable. Although many dishes seem to have been with us for hundreds of years, the detail of them – the recipes, how and when they are served, and with what accompaniment, has changed and continues to do so.

The vast majority of meals in this book were prepared in households with servants, or with outside help. Queen Victoria did not cook her own twelfth cake or roast her own beef – but nor did Mrs Cratchitt make her own cake or cook her own goose. The upper and middle classes all relied on domestic service, with a cook high on the list of priorities, and this remained true for celebratory meals well into the post-war era. Lower down the social scale use of bakers' ovens and bought puddings were quotidian and expected. The idea that one inexperienced person, working in a tiny kitchen, could plan, prepare and present a multi-course dinner from scratch without being solely focused on that task would have seemed laughable. Our Christmas dinners today are much smaller than those of the wealthy in the past, but still sometimes seem based on ideal menus drawn up in an age of cheap servants and universal home help. Dishwashers perform some of the functions of a scullery maid, but they aren't very good at grabbing pans before they burn. If we truly do cook as we claim (or as promoted by the media), we seem to be setting ourselves quite a challenge.

Attitude is important: cooking is increasingly seen as a leisure activity, not a chore, and something to be shared. For every mum who vents on social media about her family sitting in front of the TV asking when dinner is ready without offering to help, there's a happy chap basting the joint and basking in the forthcoming praise at their perfect puff pastry. Most of us are realistic about packet bread sauce and boosting the gravy with a bit of Bisto. Generational change never stops, and society moves on. Households vary, and their Christmas dinners with them.

Just as in the past, Christmas dinner is also still dependent on class. Christmas is expensive and, as in every era, those with money have more choices. A dry-hung Norfolk Bronze undoubtedly tastes better than a frozen turkey crown, just as steak-rich royal mincemeat in the nineteenth century tasted better than cowheel-based economical versions, but it will also be five times the price. Then there's the time. Christmas Eve is a working day: taking it as holiday to get ahead on the gravy is a frivolity many can't afford.

Throughout this book we've seen how varied Christmas meals have been: between eras, between classes, between regions. From the meaty sweet stews of the Tudors, to it being all about the beef, there simply isn't a standard Christmas dinner. Certainly, some foods have a very long association with Christmas – mince pies, turkey, plum pudding and cake – but the way they've been cooked has changed enormously, and their significance at Christmas has too. While some might have been present on tables 500 years ago, they've been surrounded by a huge variety of other dishes, some of which we still eat, occasionally or throughout the year. Other yuletide favourites are more recent: potatoes were only popularised in the late eighteenth century, and they rarely appeared roasted on the Christmas table until the 1950s. Christmas confectionery is a twentieth-century tale, while pigs in blankets are, in Christmas terms, a positive usurper. We've lost as well as gained. Christmas-flavoured crisps do not make up for the forgotten glories of the twelfth cake, and novelty jellied sweets aren't in the same league as regional gingerbreads, doughs and cheap buns for excited small children.

We have always used food to show who we are, and

we have always judged others by what they consume. The apparent uniformity of the modern Christmas dinner is a myth. The stories we weave about the foods we choose to eat are just that – stories – and the foods themselves are a conscious choice. There is nothing wrong with roasting a turkey and calling it traditional. Equally, there is nothing intrinsically un-Christmassy about eating pizza or going down the pub. History doesn't teach, as such, but we can nevertheless learn. Christmas dinner is about far more than the food. It's deeply individual: a mixture of family, religion, commercialism, big fires, silliness, peacefulness and charity. The English Christmas has spread well beyond Britain's own borders, transcending its pagan, then Christian, roots, and taking on a mythology of its own. Whatever we want to eat, there's probably a precedent somewhere, some time. Whether you are rich or poor, with family, friends or alone with a good book, Christmas should be only what you want it to be. And as for dinner – it is there to be enjoyed. Eat what you want, how you want, from whenever you want, and raise a glass to all the people who've done exactly that in the past.

MY CHRISTMAS DINNER (2020)

Breakfast

Mincemeat omelette (flambéed, of course)

Lunch

2 wood-fired pizzas:
Pork sausage meat, prunes and chestnuts
Spam and pineapple

Salad

Christmas cake with cheese

Supper

Fried Christmas pudding and Nesselrode ice cream

Selected bibliography

You'll find books I've merely referenced in passing in the chapter endnotes. The major works I've used, both primary and secondary, are listed here.

COOKERY AND RECIPE TEXTS

'A Lady', *London Cookery and Complete Domestic Guide* (London, George Virtue, 1836).

Acton, Eliza, *Modern Cookery in all its Branches* (London, Longman, Brown, Green & Longmans, 1849, first published 1845).

Anon, *The English and French cook describing the best and newest ways of ordering and dressing all sorts of flesh, fish and fowl, whether boiled, baked, stewed, roasted, broiled, frigassied, fryed, souc'd, marrinated, or pickled; with their proper sauces and garnishes: together with all manner of the most approved soops and potages used, either in England or France* (London, 1674).

Anon, *The Court & kitchin of Elizabeth, commonly called Joan Cromwel the wife of the late usurper* (London, 1664).

Anon, *The Gentlewomans Cabinet Unlocked* (London, 1675).

Beeton, Isabella, *The Book of Household Management* (London, Ward, Lock & Co., 1888, first published 1861).

Bradley, Richard, *The Country Housewife, and Lady's Director* (London, 1728).

Briggs, Richard, *The English Art of Cookery* (London, 1794).

Brown, Cora, Rose Brown and Bob Brown, *10,000 Snacks* (New York, Farrar & Rinehart, 1937).

Carmichael, Frances, *Cooking for Christmas* (London, Convoy, 1949).

Carter, Charles, *The Compleat City and Country Cook* (London, 1732).

Cassell & Company, *Cassell's Dictionary of Cookery* (London, Cassell, 1892).

Cooper, Joseph, *The art of cookery refin'd and augmented* (London, 1654).

Cordon Bleu, *The Cordon Bleu Cookery Course* (London, Purnell in association with the Cordon Bleu Cookery School, 1970).

Cottingham Taylor, D. D., *Economical Cookery* (London, *Daily Express*, n.d. *c.*1950).

Cradock, Fanny, *Fanny Cradock's Christmas Cookery* (Wolfe Publishing in association with the BBC, 1975).

Craig, Elizabeth, *The Way to a Good Table: Electric Cookery* (London, The British Electrical Development Association, 1937).

Craig, Elizabeth, *Cooking in Wartime* (Glasgow, The Literary Press, 1941).

Craig, Elizabeth, *Banana Dishes* (London, Herbert Jenkins, 1962).

Fairclough, Mary, *The Ideal Cookery Book* (London, Routledge, 1911).

Fettiplace, Elinor and Hilary Spurling, *Elinor Fettiplace's receipt book: Elizabethan country house cooking* (London, Viking Salamander, 1986).

Francatelli, Charles Elmé, *The Royal English and Foreign Confectioner* (London, Chapman and Hall, 1862).

Francatelli, Charles Elmé, *The Modern Cook* (London, 1846).

Garrett, Theodore, *The Encyclopaedia of Practical Cookery* (London, L. Upcott Gill, 8 vols, *c.*1895).

Glasse, Hannah, *The Art of Cookery Made Plain and Easy* (London, 1747).

Good Housekeeping, *Cooking for Christmas* (London, Guild Publishing/Ebury, 1985).

Gouffé, Jules and Alphonse Gouffé, *The Royal Cookery Book* (London, Low & Marston, 1869).

Griffiths, Annie E., *Cre-Fydd's Family Fare* (London, 1864).

Hoffmann, E. W., *Cyclopedia of Foods* (London, c.1890).

Jack, Florence B., *Cookery for Every Household* (London & Edinburgh, Thomas Nelson & Sons, 1938).

Jenks, James, *The Complete Cook* (London, 1768).

Jerome, Helen, *Concerning Cake Making* (London, Pitman, 1932).

Kent, Elizabeth Grey, Countess of, *A True Gentlewomans Delight* (London, 1653).

Kirk, M. E. W., *Tried Favourites* (Edinburgh & London, J. B. Fairgrieve & Co/Horace Marshall & Son, 1929).

Kirkland, John, *The Modern Baker, Confectioner & Caterer* (London, 1909).

Lacam, Pierre, *La Mémorial Historique et Géographique de la Pâtisserie* (Paris, 1902).

Marshall Cavendish, *Christmas Microwave Know-How* (London, Marshall Cavendish, 1985).

May, Robert, *The Accomplisht Cook* (London, 1685, first published 1660).

Mellish, Katherine, *Cookery and Domestic Management* (London, E. & F. N. Spon, 1901).

Mollard, John, *The Art of Cookery made Easy and Refined* (London, 1803).

Nott, John, *The Cook's and Confectioner's Dictionary; or, the Accomplish'd Housewife's Companion* (London, 1723).

Patten, Marguerite, *Cookery in Colour* (London, Paul Hamlyn, 1960).

Payne, Arthur G., *The Housekeeper's Guide to Preserved Meats, Fruits, Vegetables &c.* (London, Crosse & Blackwell, c.1886).

Rabisha, William, *The Whole Body of Cookery Dissected* (London, 1661).

Rycraft, Ann, *'A Ragoo of Ducks': Household Recipes from York Manuscripts* (York, The Worker's Educational Association (York Branch), 1997).

Schloesser, Frank, *The Cult of the Chafing Dish* (London, 1904).

Senn, Charles Herman, *The Century Cookbook: Practical Gastronomy and Recherché Cookery* (London, Ward, Lock & Co., 1904).

Shearson, Errol, *The Book of Vegetable Cookery* (London, Frederick Warne, 1931).

Simmons, Amelia, *American Cookery* (Hartford, 1796).

Simpson, John, *A Complete System of Cookery* (London, 1807).

Smith, Delia, *How to Cheat at Cooking* (London, Ebury, 1971).

Smith, Delia, *Delia Smith's Christmas* (London, Ebury, 1990).

Spry, Constance and Rosemary Hume, *The Constance Spry cookery book* (London, J.M. Dent & Sons, 1956, later published as Spry, C. and R. Hume, *The Constance Spry Cookery Book*, London, The Cookery Book Club, 1967).

Stewart, Katie, *Katie Stewart's Cookbook* (London, Gollancz, 1983).

Suzanne, Alfred, *La Cuisine et Pâtisserie Anglaise et Américaine* (Paris, 1904).

Tretheway, Yvonne, *Successful Cooking: What to Buy and How to Cook It* (London, *Country Life*, 1961).

Vine, Frederick, *Saleable Shop Goods* (London, c.1935).

Woolley, Hannah, *The Queen-like Closet* (London, 1670).

CHRISTMAS BOOKS

Brown, Mike, *Christmas on the Home Front* (Stroud, Sutton, 2004).

Connelly, Mark, *Christmas: A History* (London, Taurus, 2012).

Flanders, Judith, *Christmas: A Biography* (London, Picador, 2016).

Frodsham, Paul, *From Stonehenge to Santa Claus: The Evolution of Christmas* (Stroud, History, 2008).

Henisch, Bridget. A., *Cakes and Characters* (London, Prospect, 1984).

Leach, Helen, Mary Browne and Raelene Inglis, *The Twelve Cakes of Christmas: an Evolutionary History with Recipes* (Dunedin, Otago University Press, 2011).

Pimlott, John, *The Englishman's Christmas* (Hassocks, Harvester Press, 1978).

Shanahan, Madeline, *Christmas Food & Feasting: A History* (London, Rowman & Littlefield, 2019).

Weightman, Gavin and Steve Humphries, *Christmas Past* (London, Sidgwick & Jackson for LWT, 1988).

Notes

1   Alfred Suzanne, *La Cuisine et Pâtisserie Anglaise et Américaine* (Paris, 1904), pp. 365–6.

2   Mark Connelly, *Christmas: A History* (London, Taurus, 2012); Judith Flanders, *Christmas: A Biography* (London, Picador, 2016).

3   *John Russell's Book of Nurture*, cited in Peter Brears, *Cooking and Dining in Medieval England* (Totnes, Prospect, 2008), p. 380.

4   Bridget Ann Henisch, *Fast and Feast: Food in Medieval Society* (Philadelphia, Pennsylvania University Press, 1976), p. 47.

5   Cited in Lauren Johnson, *So Great a Prince: England in 1509* (London, Head of Zeus, 2016), p. 157.

6   Anon, *A True Accompt of The Most Triumphant and Royal Accomplishment of the Baptism of the Most Excellent, Right High and Mighty Prince Henry Frederick (etc)* (London, 1603).

7   Paul Frodsham, *From Stonehenge to Santa Claus: The Evolution of Christmas* (Stroud, History, 2008), p. 140.

8   *Ibid.*, p. 141.

9   Theodore Garrett, *The Encyclopedia of Practical Cookery* (London, L. Upcott Gill, *c.*1895), p. 383.

10   Charles Elmé Francatelli, *The Modern Cook* (London, 1846).

11   John Kirkland, *The Modern Baker, Confectioner & Caterer* (London, 1909).

12   Charles Elmé Francatelli, *The Royal English and Foreign Confectioner* (London, Chapman and Hall, 1862), pp. 292–4.

13   Robert May, *The Accomplisht Cook* (London, 1660).

14   In Britain we mainly heard about the burgers, but horse was also relabelled and sold as beef for filling cheap merguez sausages.

15   Mary Fairclough, *The Ideal Cookery Book* (London, Routledge, 1911).

16   Cora, Rose and Bob Brown, *10,000 Snacks* (New York, Farrar & Rinehart, 1937), pp. 18, 189; L. Murphy, https://separatedbyacommonlanguage.blogspot.com/2020/02/pigs-in-blankets.html (2020).

17   Marguerite Patten, *Cookery in Colour* (London, Paul Hamlyn, 1960); *Good Housekeeping, Cooking For Christmas* (London, Guild Publishing/Ebury, 1985).

18   Hannah Woolley, *The Queen-like Closet* (London, 1670), p. 194.

19   Mainly Anon, *The English and French Cook* (London, 1674); J. Cooper, *The art of cookery refin'd and augmented* (London, 1654); Anon, *The Court & kitchin of Elizabeth, commonly called Joan Cromwel the wife of the late usurper* (London, 1664).

20   Elizabeth Grey, Countess of Kent, *A True Gentlewomans Delight* (London, 1653), p. 82.

21   Peter Brears, *Cooking and Dining in Tudor and Early Stuart England* (Totnes, Prospect, 2015), p. 166.

22   Thomas Tusser, *Five hundreth points of good husbandry united to as many of good huswiferie* (1573), ch. 26.

23   Ivan Day, 'Drop the Shaped Minc'd Pies' at http://foodhistorjottings.blogspot.com/2011/12/drop-shaped-mincd-pies.html (2011).

24   Ivan Day, 'Shaped Minc'd Pies Again', at http://foodhistorjottings.blogspot.com/2011/12/shaped-mincd-pies-again.html (2011).

25 Mary Anne Dixon (and daughters?), unpublished manuscript recipe book (n.d.), York City Archives, Dixon family papers, Acc. 135 box 12. Thank you to Laura Yeoman at the YCA for sending me a copy of the recipe.

26 Frances Carmichael, *Cooking for Christmas* (London, Convoy, 1949), p. 70, which includes a version made with beef and beef stock – though the stock can apparently be substituted (slightly incongruously) with pineapple juice.

27 Fanny Cradock, *Fanny Cradock's Christmas Cookery* (Wolfe Publishing in association with the BBC, 1975). The snowball is in the *Radio Times*, 8 Dec 1966, with huge thanks to Kevin Geddes for sending me the relevant page.

28 Eleanor Fettiplace and Hilary Spurling, *Elinor Fettiplace's receipt book: Elizabethan country house cooking* (London, Viking Salamander, 1986).

29 York Archives, Minster Library, Hailstone Collection QQ5, reprinted in Ann Rycraft, *'A Ragoo of Ducks': Household Recipes from York Manuscripts* (York, The Worker's Educational Association (York Branch), 1997), p. 63.

30 In author's collection, rather mouse-eaten and with bonus drawing of a horse.

31 Laura Mason, 'Prodigal frugality: Yorkshire pudding and parkin, two traditional Yorkshire foods', *Traditional Food East and West of the Pennines* (Stroud, Sutton, 1994), pp. 143–86.

32 John Ashton, et al., *A righte merrie Christmasse!!! The story of Christ-tide. [With] copper-plate etching of The wassail song* (London, Leadenhall Press, etc., 1894), ch. 22.

33 'Traditional Fare', in *The Yorkshire Post & Leeds Intelligencier*, 5 January 1954.

34 Sam Bilton, *First Catch Your Gingerbread* (London, Prospect, 2020).

35 RA VIC/MAIN/QVJ (W) 24th December 1833 (Queen Victoria's handwriting).

36 RA VIC/MAIN/QVJ (W) 24th December 1856 (Princess Beatrice's copies).

37 Wellcome Library MS1842, recipe 106. Accessed at https://wellcomelibrary.org/item/b19102689#?c=0&m=0&s=0&cv=33&z=-0.3027%2C0.0332%2C1.6703%2C1.105 December 2021.

38 Elisha Coles, *An English Dictionary* (London, 1677); Edward Phillips, *The New World of English Words* (London, 1658).

39 Ivan Day, 'Some Christmas night-caps', at http://foodhistorjottings.blogspot.com/2013/12/some-christmas-nightcaps.html (2013), accessed November 2020.

40 *London Courier and Evening Gazette*, 6 January 1801.

41 John Nott, *The Cook's and Confectioner's Dictionary; or, the Accomplish'd Housewife's Companion* (London, 1723).

42 Robert May, *The Accomplisht Cook, or The art and mystery of cookery* (1660).

43 Phillip Stubbes, *The Anatomie of Abuses, Part I* (London, 1583), pages unnumbered, image 114.

44 Robert Fletcher, 'Christmas Day', quoted in J. Brand, *Observations on Popular Antiquities, vol 1.* (London, 1877), p. 284.

45 John Taylor, *Christmas In & Out* (London, 1652), no page given.

46 John Evelyn and Richard Bray (eds.), *The Diary of John Evelyn,* Vol 1. (London, 1901), p. 319, accessed via https://www.gutenberg.org/files/41218/41218-h/41218-h.htm.

47 John (J.A.R.) Pimlott, *The Englishman's Christmas* (Hassocks, Harvester Press, 1978), p. 58.

48 May, *The Accomplisht Cook, or The art and mystery of cookery* (1660).

49   Garrett, *The Encyclopedia of Practical Cookery*.

50   Stephen Trigg, *Most strange and terrible astrological predictions and dreadful presages for the ensuing year* (London, 1684).

51   Frodsham, *From Stonehenge to Santa Claus: The Evolution of Christmas*, p. 153.

52   Pimlott, *The Englishman's Christmas*, p. 69.

53   Ashton, et al., *A Righte Merrie Christmasse!!!*

54   Janet C. Scott, *Simple Home Cookery* (Brown & Polson Cookery Service leaflet, 1934); Kaori O'Connor, 'The King's Christmas pudding: globalization, recipes, and the commodities of empire', in *Journal of Global History* 4 (2009), 127–55.

55   Charles Carter, *The compleat city and country cook: or, accomplish'd housewife. Containing several hundred of the most approv'd receipts … To which is added … near two hundred … receipts in physick, etc.* (1732).

56   Richard Bradley, *The Country Housewife, and Lady's Director* (London, 1728).

57   John R. Smith, *A Dictionary of Archaic and Provincial Words* (London, 1847), vol. 1, p. 427.

58   Thomas K. Hervey, *The Book of Christmas … With Illustrations by R. Seymour* (London, 1836), p. 276.

59   Richard Briggs, *The English Art of Cookery* (London, 1791).

60   Rebecca Harris-Quigg and me, respectively.

61   Helen Saberi and A. Davidson, *Trifle* (Totnes, Prospect, 2009).

62   Garrett, *The Encyclopedia of Practical Cookery*, p. 613.

63   Constance Spry and Rosemary Hume, *The Constance Spry cookery book* (London, J.M. Dent & Sons., 1956), p. 956.

64   https://www.seriouseats.com/2014/05/the-serious-eats-guide-to-british-sweets.html.

65 https://www.mercotte.fr/2018/10/03/le-trifle-royal-le-
    meilleur-patissier-saison-7-emission-4-god-save-the-cakes/
    – you couldn't make it up.

66 Cassell & Company, *Cassell's Dictionary of Cookery* (London,
    Cassell, 1892), p. 136.

67 Kevin Geddes, *It's all in the Booklet: Festive Fun with Fanny
    Cradock* (Fantom, 2019), p. 35.

68 Eliza Acton, *Modern Cookery in all its Branches* (London,
    Longman, Brown, Green & Longmans, 1849), p. 444.

69 John Simpson, *A Complete System of Cookery* (London, 1807).

70 Jules Gouffé and Alphonse Gouffé, *The Royal Cookery Book*
    (London, Low & Marston, 1869), p. 540. The 16° refers to the
    sugar concentration, to be measured on a saccharometer using
    the Brix scale. This is very much a professional recipe.

71 It has also been the subject of some debate. It was first
    published in English in 1836 in a translation of Antonin
    Carême's *L'Art de la Cuisine Française*, wherein he took credit
    for its invention. When Eliza Acton copied it into her best-
    selling *Modern Cookery* in 1845, she attributed it to Carême,
    admitting she trusted him so much that she hadn't felt the need
    to test it. Her text was widely plagiarised, esepcially by
    Beeton, and Carême has been the acknowledged inventor of
    the dish ever since. However, in his original (French) text
    Carême admits that the recipe was invented by a man called
    Mony, chef to Count Nesselrode – hence the name (though
    Carême claims it was in turn inspired by his own chestnut
    pudding). A generation later, Jules Gouffé, who had trained
    under Carême and knew Mony as a friend, published his
    version of the recipe, stating simply that he'd got it from the
    source – Mony.

72 25 Dec 1776. James Woodforde, *The Diary of a Country Parson
    1758–1802* (Oxford, OUP, 1978).

73   c.1826, letter to Bernard Barton, in Charles Lamb and Mary
     Lamb, *Works of Charles and Mary Lamb. VI-VII. Letters*
     (1905), accessed via https://www.lordbyron.org/monograph.
     php?doc=ChLamb.1905&select=L1826.

74   Victoire, Count de Soligny, 1823, cited at https://www.
     futurelearn.com/info/courses/royal-food/0/steps/36813.

75   Edward Holt on George III, cited at https://www.futurelearn.
     com/info/courses/royal-food/0/steps/36813.

76   'A Lady', *London Cookery and Complete Domestic Guide*
     (London, George Virtue, 1836), p. 492. For more on the cow
     thing, see Ivan Day, 'Further musings on syllabub' (1996),
     available at https://www.historicfood.com/Syllabubs%20
     Essay.pdf.

77   Depending on who you read, the quote is attributed either to
     Voltaire or Francesco Caracciolo, the Neapolitan Ambassador
     to Britain (the latter rings truer, given he was writing in the
     1790s).

78   Arthur G. Payne, *The Housekeeper's Guide to Preserved Meats,
     Fruits, Vegetables &c.* (London, Crosse & Blackwell, c.1886).
     The primitive nature of it comes from A. Suzanne, A., *La
     Cuisine et Pâtisserie Anglaise et Américaine* (Paris, 1904), p. 290
     – but his version is also heavily bastardised, being essentially
     melted butter, pan juice and one of the many equivalents to
     Worcestershire sauce.

79   Anon, *The Gentlewomans Cabinet Unlocked* (London, 1675), no
     page given.

80   Richard Bradley, *The Country Housewife, and Lady's Director*
     (London, 1728), p. 133.

81   Ashton, et al., *A righte merrie Christmasse!!!*

82   Roger Manning, 'Unlawful hunting in England, 1500–1640', in
     Forest and Conservation History, 38 (1), (1994), pp. 16–23.

83   *The Lady's Magazine* (London, 1780), p. 682.

84 Hannah Glasse, *The Art of Cookery Made Plain and Easy* (London, 1747), p. 73. Glasse also coined the phrase Yorkshire pudding, for what had previously been known as batter or fire pudding, but the exact connection with Yorkshire isn't known.

85 John Sykes, *Local Records*, Vol 1. (1883), p. 270, available at https://books.google.co.uk/books?id=--lFAQAAIAAJ&pri ntsec=frontcover&source=gbs_ge_summary_r&cad=0#v=0 nepage&q&f=false

86 Charles Dickens, *The Holly-Tree Inn* (London, 1885), p. 17. Via https://archive.org/details/hollytreeinnpictoodick/ page/n27/mode/2up.

87 Florence B. Jack, *Cookery for Every Household* (London & Edinburgh, Thomas Nelson & Sons, 1938), pp. 307–9.

88 Cradock, *Fanny Cradock's Christmas Cookery*.

89 Pimlott, *The Englishman's Christmas*, p. 87.

90 Agatha Christie, *The Adventure of the Christmas Pudding* (London, Collins, 1960), p. 7.

91 Shanahan, Madeline, *Christmas Food & Feasting: A History* (London, Rowman & Littlefield, 2019), p. 84, citing Marcus Clarke (1855).

92 George Bernard Shaw, in *Music in London, 1890–94*, Vol. III (1893), p. 113, 20 December 1893, cited at http:// shawquotations.blogspot.com/2016/12/christmas-is-forced-upon-reluctant-and.html.

93 Annie E. Griffiths, *Cre-Fydd's Family Fare* (London, 1864), p. 137.

94 Cassell & Company, *Cassell's Dictionary of Cookery*. Personally I find this ludicrously sweet, but I've been firmly told that while it is, indeed, tooth-meltingly sugary, that is very nice, thank you, and I shouldn't change it.

95 Frank Schloesser, *The Cult of the Chafing Dish* (London, 1904), p. 9.

96 J. W. Hoffman, *Cyclopedia of Foods* (London, *c*.1890).

97 Errol Shearson, *The Book of Vegetable Cookery* (London, Frederick Warne, 1930), p. 85.

98 RA MRH/MRHF/MENUS/WC/1855: 25 December. This was for 30 people. À la Palfy probably denotes use of vanilla sugar, and flamaris is a garbled spelling of flammarie, a German version of flummery and essentially a refined blancmange.

99 Daniel Defoe, *A Tour Thro' The Whole Island of Great Britain* (1724), no page given. Letter 1, part 2: Harwich & Suffolk. Accessed at https://visionofbritain.org.uk/travellers/Defoe/3.

100 Thomas Hervey, *The Book of Christmas* (1836), quoted in G. Weightman and S. Humphries, *Christmas Past* (London, Sidgwick & Jackson, 1988), for LWT.

101 Thanks to Ivan Day for an unexpected and highly enjoyable conversation on the swan industry and quite how nasty elderly swan is to eat.

102 *The Times*, 14 November 1931: kennel, farm & aviary section.

103 Thanks to John Foster for this.

104 Pierre Lacam, *La Mémorial Historique et Géographique de la Pâtisserie* (Paris, 1902); F. Vine, *Saleable Shop Goods* (London, *c*.1935).

105 Helen Jerome, *Concerning Cake Making* (London, Pitman, 1932), p. 119; Cordon Bleu, *The Cordon Bleu Cookery Course* (London, Purnell in association with the Cordon Bleu Cookery School, 1970), 37: 9

106 Peter Brears, *Traditional Food in Yorkshire* (Totnes, Prospect, 2014).

107 Garrett, *The Encyclopaedia of Practical Cookery*, p. 384.

108 Ashton, et al., *A righte merrie Christmasse!!!*

109 Peter Brears, 'Yule-doos, pop-ladies and pig-hogs' (1993), in PPC 44, 26–34.

110 *Ibid*.; Mary-Anne Boermans, 'Coventrys, Godcakes and Congleton Cakes' (2019), https://dejafood.uk/2019/09/14/coventrys-godcakes-and-congleton-cakes/ accessed December 2020.

111 Charles Senn, *The New Century Cookbook: Practical Gastronomy and Recherché Cookery* (London, Ward, Lock & Co., 1904).

112 Suzanne, *La Cuisine et Pâtisserie Anglaise et Américaine*.

113 Joyce Gibson, 'Christmas in Wartime on the BBC WW2 People's War archive' (2005), from https://www.bbc.co.uk/history/ww2peopleswar/stories/00/a5947400.shtml.

114 Mike Brown, *Christmas on the Home Front* (Stroud, Sutton, 2004), p. 120.

115 Quoted in Stuart Hylton, *Reporting the Blitz: New from the Home Front Communities* (Sutton, Stroud, 2012).

116 Elizabeth Craig, *The Way to a Good Table: Electric Cookery* (London, The British Electrical Development Association, 1937), p. 45.

117 Elizabeth Craig, *Cooking in Wartime* (Glasgow, The Literary Press, 1941), p. 102.

118 'Christmas Catalogues' at The Huntley & Palmers Collection, available at http://www.huntleyandpalmers.org.uk.

119 Carmichael, *Cooking for Christmas*, p. 77.

120 M. E. W. Kirk, *Tried Favourites* (Edinburgh & London, J.B. Fairgrieve & Co/Horace Marshall & Son, 1929), p. 267.

121 *Norwich Mercury*, 28 December 1895.

122 Simmons, *American Cookery*.

123 Griffiths, *Cre-Fydd's Family Fare*; Churchill Archives, Cambridge CSCT 9-3-2: staff menu book 1949.

124 William Rabisha, *The Whole Body of Cookery Dissected* (London, 1661), p. 198.

125 Schloesser, *The Cult of the Chafing Dish*, p. 154.

126 Katherine Mellish, *Cookery and Domestic Management* (London, E. & F. N. Spon, 1901).

127 *Good Housekeeping*, *Cooking For Christmas*; Marshall Cavendish, *Christmas Microwave Know-How* (London, Marshall Cavendish, 1985).

128 Craig, Elizabeth, *Banana Dishes* (London, Herbert Jenkins, 1962), p. 39.

129 Marshall Cavendish, *Christmas Microwave Know-How*.

130 See, for example, Oxford, cited in 'Markets and Fairs' in *Victoria County History – Oxfordshire. A History of the County of Oxford*, vol. 4, the City of Oxford, pp. 305–12, accessed at https://www.british-history.ac.uk/vch/oxon/vol4/pp305-312.

131 Helen Leach, Mary Browne and Raelene Inglis, *The Twelve Cakes of Christmas: an Evolutionary History with Recipes* (Dunedin, Otago University Press, 2011), p. 27.

132 Bridget A. Henisch, *Cakes and Characters* (London, Prospect, 1984), p. 50.

133 James Jenks, *The Complete Cook* (London, 1768), p. 246; Leach, et al., *The Twelve Cakes of Christmas*.

134 William Hone, *The Every Day Book* (London, William Hone, 1826), 6 January, accessed at http://www.gutenberg.org/files/53275/53275-h/53275-h.htm.

135 Thomas Morton, manuscript book in the author's possession (n.d., probably 1840s). Several printed books could be the source for this, though the exact wording differs – usually they state 'wholesale confectioners'.

136 Shanahan, *Christmas Food & Feasting*, p. 105.

137 Charles Dickens, *The Mystery of Edwin Drood* (1870), ch. 14.

138 E.g. Peggy Hutchinson's *North Country Cooking Secrets* (1935). I am indebted to the reliably brilliant Mary-Anne Boermans for this information.

139 Delia Smith, *How to Cheat at Cooking* (London, Ebury, 1971), p. 150.

140 Katie Stewart, *Katie Stewart's Cookbook* (London, Gollancz, 1983), accessed via https://app.ckbk.com/recipe/kati85568c10s001ss005r013/christmas-cake.

141 J. Mollard, *The Art of Cookery made Easy and Refined* (London, 1803). NB: the first edition of 1801 does not contain this recipe. Subsequent editions do.

142 Constance Spry and Rosemary Hume, *The Constance Spry Cookery Book* (London, The Cookery Book Club, 1967), p. x.

143 D. D. Cottingham Taylor, *Economical Cookery* (London, Daily Express, n.d. c.1950), p. 110.

144 'Savoury Dishes for the Special Season', *Coventry Evening Telegraph*, 6 December 1977, p. 8.

145 Yvonne Tretheway, *Successful Cooking: What to Buy and How to Cook It* (London, Country Life, 1961), p. 127.

146 Martin Caraher, Tim Lange and Paul Dixon, 'The Influence of TV and Celebrity Chefs on Public Attitudes and Behavior Among the English Public', *Journal for the Study of Food and Society* 4(1), (2000), pp. 27–46.

147 Patten, *Cookery in Colour*, no page given, recipe 937.

148 Cradock, *Fanny Cradock's Christmas Cookery*.

149 It is on BBC iPlayer and if you haven't watched it, what are you doing with your time? The booklet is virtually unobtainable, but its secrets can be found in Geddes, *It's All In the Booklet*.

150 Ellie Donnell in .delicious magazine, 20 August 2019, available at https://www.deliciousmagazine.co.uk/classic-christmas-menu/.

151 Delia Smith, *Delia Smith's Christmas* (London, Ebury, 1990), pp. 189–201.

Acknowledgements

Lots of people helped write this book, some of them unknowingly. So, to all the people who have attended my Christmas food talks, and helped me hone the interesting bits, thank you. The same goes for the people who responded so enthusiastically to my mad twitter surveys (or, you know, sent me books or extracts of books or generally wonderful things).

I wrote this during the here-there-and-everywhere-as-long-as-you-stay-home coronavirus crisis of winter 2020–21. Thank you hugely to the University of York, where I am a research associate, for enabling me to access corners of the internet I would not otherwise have access to. Special mention to Chris Johnson of IT Support, who talked me down from the ceiling when I was about to burn my computer due to Endnote issues. And thank you to the team at DeliaOnline for answering my query on editions.

Specific thanks go to Lucy Worsley for wine-fuelled chats, bangs of expectation and encouraging my wilder flights of fancy; to Regula Ysewijn for being generally brilliant, enthusiastic about my obsessions and for introducing me to fuckmylife as an all-purpose swear; to Kevin Geddes for sending me Fannytastic information; and to culinary history super-sleuth Mary Anne Boermans for furkling for recipes and sending me a recipe which actually worked for sodding pepper cake. Chris Grundy photographed the Christmas issue of *Cordon Bleu* for me and commented on what she'd actually cooked in the 1970s. Esther Wilson interned for me during the closing stages of this – she has been unflinchingly fabulous in dealing with me writing four books at once.

My agent, Tim Bates, has been a stalwart, as ever, and even in a year where beer and balmy afternoons were banned still managed to take me for a Christmas lunch with the absolute most bonkers dessert I've ever seen. I mean, WHY? WHY WAS THERE A SLEIGH? Huge and heartfelt thanks to my editor Rebecca Gray, whose idea this book was, and whose edits made me all warm and fuzzy. Thanks too, to Calah Singleton, for coping well with meeting me for the first time on a mad Victory paperback Zoom.

I'd also like to extend personal thanks to the usual motley crew: Kathy Hipperson, my partner in Xmas food crime, recipe tester and fellow mincemeat enthusiast; Bex and Charlie Harris-Quigg for eating the cake (again, soz); Laura Gale for buoying me up from a suitable (if saddening) social distance; Kristy Noble for the big book exchange and Rebecca Lane and Katherine and Rich Boardman-Hims for over a year of gin & crisps via Zoom. Not only was it sanity-giving but they are responsible for stuffing and leftovers being separate chapters. Also, I wrote the introduction while on Zoom to them. I'd also like to thank Mike and Angela Gray, plus enormous thanks to Richard Gray and Jess Smith for the Saturday Dinner challenges – and so much else.

Finally, as ever and always, thank you to Matt Howling. You can now finish that cake.

List of Illustrations

Index

Page references for notes are followed by n